Your Machine's Decorative Stitches

Karen Linduska

American Quilter's Society
P. O. Box 3290 • Paducah, KY 42002-3290
www.AmericanQuilter.com

Located in Paducah, Kentucky, the American Quilter's Society (AQS) is dedicated to promoting the accomplishments of today's quilters. Through its publications and events, AQS strives to honor today's quiltmakers and their work and to inspire future creativity and innovation in quiltmaking.

EXECUTIVE BOOK EDITOR: ANDI MILAM REYNOLDS
SENIOR BOOK EDITOR: LINDA BAXTER LASCO
COPY EDITOR: CHRYSTAL ABHALTER
GRAPHIC DESIGN: ELAINE WILSON
COVER DESIGN: MICHAEL BUCKINGHAM
PHOTOGRAPHY: CHARLES R. LYNCH

Additional copies of this book may be ordered from the American Quilter's Society, PO Box 3290, Paducah, KY 42002-3290, or online at www.AmericanQuilter.com.

Text © 2011, Author, Karen Linduska
Artwork © 2011, American Quilter's Society

Library of Congress Cataloging-in-Publication Data

Linduska, Karen.
  Your machine's decorative stitches / by Karen Linduska.
    p. cm.
  ISBN 978-1-57432-645-1
  1. Machine quilting--Patterns. 2. Stitches (Sewing) I. Title.
  TT835.L538 2011
  646.2'044--dc22

                          2011008185

TITLE PAGE:
CATTAILS WITH DRAGONFLIES, detail. Full project on pages 76–79.

RIGHT:
GARDEN PARTY, detail. Full project on pages 58–63.

Dedication

To my best friend and partner in life, Tim, and to all my four-legged family members past, present, and future who make my life complete.

Acknowledgments

Jerry Stefl & M. Joan Lintault, my teachers, who nurtured the foundation of my work.

Tim Linduska for the stitch artwork.

My students, who constantly surprise me.

Chuck and Steve at Calico Country in Carbondale, Illinois—many thanks for everything.

Tim and Don, you are my family.

Sue, for watching my back.

Jimmy Allen, I miss you.

Steve Jeffery, Chris Tryon, and Larry Spoon from Baby Lock—thank you for sponsoring me with the Ellisimo. It is a wonderful machine and perfect for this process.

Fairfield, for sponsoring me with Low-Loft® Poly Batting.

YLI Threads, for sponsoring me with Variations Thread.

Thread Art, for sponsoring me with stabilizer, needles, and pre-wound bobbins.

Contents

✳✳✳✳✳✳✳✳✳✳✳✳✳✳✳✳✳✳

LEFT:
FOREST FROLIC, detail. Full project on pages 88–93.

How to Use These Projects......33

✳✳✳✳✳✳✳✳✳✳✳✳✳✳✳✳✳✳✳✳

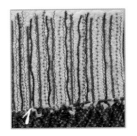
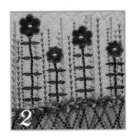

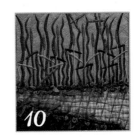

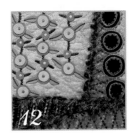

Introduction

If you have a sewing machine with the built-in decorative stitches and you don't know what to do with them,

"THIS IS THE BOOK FOR YOU!"

Welcome to my world of color, thread, and decorative stitch machine embroidery. This process can be done on any sewing machine that has a significant number of built-in decorative stitches. Any stitch can create surface design. With my technique I use as many stitches as possible. I don't do anything in the traditional way. So be prepared to push the envelope.

I will show you how to alter both decorative and utility stitches. We will take the fear and guesswork out of using your sewing machine and its manual. The best way to get the most out of this book is to read all the information and do the projects in the order they're presented. Each one leads to the next.

The Birth of Decorative Stitch Threadwork

It was in college where I learned to create surface design. This was a new art form back in the late 1970s. I was using a Sears Kenmore machine with only 10 utility stitches. I used wax paper as a stabilizer. This was the foundation for my work today.

Over the years my fiber art went in several directions, always moving forward, looking for my voice, always asking myself, "What if?" In 1998 I bought my first decorative stitch sewing machine. It was the magic tool and opened up a whole new world for me. I spent the next five years learning the machine, exploring different ideas, and pushing myself.

In 2001 I started working on a series called Rebuilding the Wall on My Terms. It is a series of 10 art quilts about creative spiritual recovery. The fifth quilt had an intense subject matter and was very technical. I was looking for something fun to do after I finished this piece. I started to play with painting fabric and then fabric dyeing. I liked the results and started to stitch on the painted fabric with my machine's built-in decorative stitches. In 2004, using the layered fabric painting technique I discovered and my decorative stitch thread painting technique, my Fantasy Garden series was born. I gave myself plenty of time to explore and play with the machine. I gave myself time to make mistakes. Some projects were dismal failures, but I learned something from them anyway.

WHAT IS DECORATIVE STITCH THREADWORK?

Decorative stitch threadwork uses any of the built-in utility and decorative stitches to create surface design. Altering the stitches allows you to draw with them.

HOW IS IT DONE?

This is a wholecloth process. Everything is layered on the foundation fabric and built up from there. I call this style of work abstract realism. So remember this when working on these images. The abstract part will free you up to just go with the shapes. The realism will bring in an element of reality. Also there is a funky element. When you put all this together it creates a very fun style.

This is a layering process from start to finish. The foundation fabric is the beginning layer. Remember we are not going for perfection. You will distort on purpose. Allow the stitches to come out as they will. This will free you up to just play and have fun. Some of the stitches will be covered with other layers. This will also add depth to your piece.

Most sewing machines with built-in decorative stitches have a maximum width of 5mm–9mm. Because of this, your stitches may not look exactly like mine. The images of the stitches I have provided in this lesson are a maximum of 7mm wide.

This process is done with the feed dogs UP. Lowering the feed dogs will totally distort the decorative stitch. This is a technique that I will talk about later.

WHAT STITCHES CAN CREATE SURFACE DESIGN?

You can create surface design with ANY stitch, from the straight running stitch to the most detailed decorative one. Look at the stitches for their design quality, not for their intended function. Even the utility stitches can be beautiful when used in a creative way.

WHAT IF MY STITCHES AREN'T PERFECT?

We're not going for perfection. I learned early on that the only way to make the decorative stitches perfect is to run them through an embroidery hoop. I did not want to be limited this way, so I decided just to let the stitches come out as they would. This was very freeing. It allowed me to just play and go funky. I've learned that if you do this all over an art quilt, it works. This is what I mean by not going for perfection. I use rough edges on the fabric. I don't worry about puckering. I let the bobbin thread show. I don't worry about loose threads or skipped stitches. I allow the stitches to distort.

I only have one rule: You must use stabilizer. I make my stabilizer slightly larger than my foundation piece so I can run my stitches off the fabric onto the stabilizer. When the final piece is cropped, the stitches will run right to the edge of the piece.

Free Up Your Inner Five-Year-Old

If you give five-year-olds a large sheet of blank paper and a box of crayons they do not have a problem with not being perfect. They just go at the paper with a free abandonment. That is what I want you to do. It will seem like there is a lot of technical information in the beginning of this book. But what this process really is all about is playing and drawing with the stitch. There is an exercise in the beginning of the projects that will help you deal with freeing up your inner five-year-old. I recommend you do this exercise. It will help you to get familiar with the movements and the stitches.

Most of all, have fun!

Getting Started

The Sewing Machine

Your local sewing machine dealer is there for you. Tell them your interests. Test different sewing machines before you buy. They are all different. They all have wonderful features. Find one that works for you. Once you have purchased this machine, take a class on how to use it. I can't stress this enough. After the class, go home and play. Don't start some big project that will overwhelm you. Start small and just get the feel of the machine. Make some small pieces that might not even have a purpose except just to learn and play. Do a sampler. Try to get on the machine as much as you can. Lock yourself in your sewing room with a "Do Not Disturb" sign on the door if you have to.

One year later, take another class on your machine. The first time you take the class you will learn the basic information. The second time you take the class you will absorb more information and tips about its extra features. I am all about absorbing as much as I can.

If you are lucky enough to have a local sewing center, please support it. They are wonderful places to visit and get creative ideas. In this day of online shopping, it is easy to forget these special places. If you want them to be there for you, support them.

SERVICING YOUR MACHINE

Keeping your machine in top working condition is very important. Have it professionally serviced on a regular basis, at least once a year.

MAIN FUNCTIONS WE WILL USE

I can guide you on the basics but remember that all machines are different. You need to rely on your machine's manual for the fine tuning. Don't be afraid to change the settings on the stitches. They are meant to be altered. That is why the settings are there. You may or may not have some or any of the special features. Do not worry about this. The special features make the process move faster but they are not a requirement. You can still do almost everything manually.

USING YOUR MANUAL

Read your manual. It has tons of information that you may not even think of. You spent a lot of money on your machine and reading the manual is a way to get the most out of this great tool. At first just glance through it and look at the captions and pictures. Then go back and slowly go through. Highlight the areas that interest you. Go back again and read over those areas. Take notes if you want. I keep my manual where I sit at night to watch TV. I try to pick it up and look at it a few times a week and I keep a note pad nearby.

Some of the features we will use in this process are in the "internal workings" of the machine—how to adjust the level of the presser foot, for example, if it is adjustable. Information will be in the main functions section. This is part of learning to use your machine more efficiently. Ask your sewing machine dealer if you have trouble with anything. That is part of the service they provide.

Find the section about getting ready or overview. This is in the front of the book. Read all of the introductory overview to learn the operations of the machine. Read about key functions. Knowing most of these functions is vital in altering the stitches. Next check out the section about the utility stitches. You will be amazed how pretty some of them are. Think about them as design, not function. Ask yourself what this stitch would look like stitched all over a surface. Next find the sections about the built-in decorative stitches and about editing stitch patterns. This is how you alter the stitches.

Find the pages that have pictures of the stitches—all of the stitches. Mark them or print them out. I keep a printout of my machine's stitches on my wall so I can see them.

Terminology

Altered stitches—stitches sewn differently from the default settings or manually distorted stitches

Back-to-back stitches—two rows of stitches with one straight edge are stitched so the straight edges are together and the uneven edges face away from each other (The grass stitch is a good choice for back-to-back stitching.)

Background stitching—quilting that is done to prepare the foundation fabric for the decorative stitching

Couching—stitching down yarn with a topstitch

Default setting—the standard way your machine sews a selected stitch

Foundation fabric—the main wholecloth fabric to be used for your art quilt

Ground level—the line between the ground fabric and the foundation fabric on the upper part of the quilt

Internal workings—the main workings of the sewing machine. There are functions that can be changed to suit your needs.

Layering stitches—stitching over already stitched areas, either right on top of existing stitches or offset slightly

Offset—stitching next to and not quite aligned with the previous stitching, making sure you are not on top of the existing stitches

Push faster—while sewing, push the fabric with an even pressure faster than the feed dogs are moving it to allow the stitch to distort slightly

Sandwich—several layers of materials stacked together

Stacking stitches—sewing stitches right next to each other to create a solid pattern

Test sheet—a sample sandwich to test your stitching before trying it on your project

Stitch Information
ANATOMY OF A STITCH

Ask yourself where the stitch pattern starts and where it ends. Which direction does it go? Does it stitch out straight or does it have a curve? A straight stitch pierces the fabric at the beginning and the end of the stitch. Simple decorative stitches pierce the fabric several times from the beginning to the end. The more detailed the decorative stitch, the more the needle pierces the fabric. Keep this in mind when selecting thread weights. Some thicker threads or metallics sometimes do not work well on the very detailed stitches.

HOW TO USE THE STITCH IMAGES

There is a drawing of each of the 28 stitches used in the projects. They are basic, built-in utility and decorative stitches. Most of the sewing machines made in the last 10 years should have these stitches or something similar. All you have to do is match the drawing to one of the stitches in your machine. If you do not have that EXACT stitch select one that is SIMILAR. Your stitches don't have to be exactly like mine. This is a free-form process. There is no wrong way to do it. It is all about having fun.

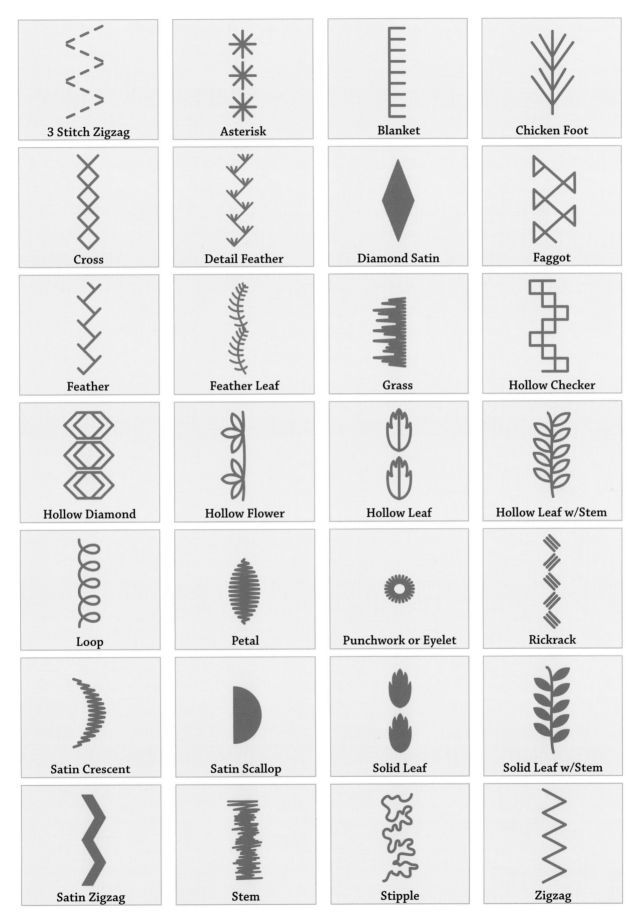

3 Stitch Zigzag

Asterisk

Blanket

Chicken Foot

Cross

Detail Feather

Diamond Satin

Faggot

Feather

Feather Leaf

Grass

Hollow Checker

Hollow Diamond

Hollow Flower

Hollow Leaf

Hollow Leaf w/Stem

Loop

Petal

Punchwork or Eyelet

Rickrack

Satin Crescent

Satin Scallop

Solid Leaf

Solid Leaf w/Stem

Satin Zigzag

Stem

Stipple

Zigzag

HOLLOW STITCHES AND SOLID STITCHES

A hollow stitch is an outline of a shape. These are perfect for the background plants. You can color in the hollow shapes with fabric markers, to make them appear to be a solid shape. A solid stitch is a totally filled shape. These are the satin stitches.

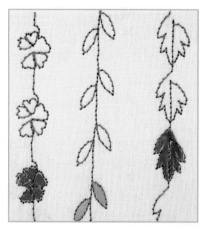

Hollow stitches colored in with fabric markers

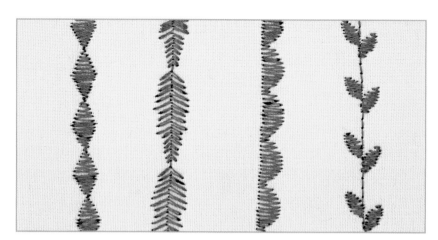

Solid stitches

SINGLE STITCH SETTING

With the single stitch feature, the machine will stitch out only one motif. It will automatically tie off at the beginning and end of the motif. This is a great feature to use with my process. It will give you more control over the stitch. Without the single stitch feature, it is very easy to start stitching into the next stitch pattern. Most of the newer sewing machines have the single stitch function. Check your manual. If you do not have this feature, you will need to pay more attention to the ending of the stitch and stop before the next motif starts.

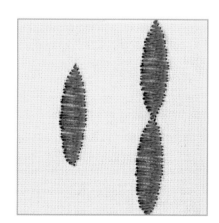

Single stitch examples

DEFAULT SETTING

When you select a stitch, any computerized machine will automatically set the optimum variables for the stitch—length, width, and so on. That's the default setting. Non-computerized machines will usually provide the default setting information in the instruction manual. Any altering of the stitch will be done from this point. If you change the stitch in a way you are not happy with, simply revert to the default setting. Some machines have a reset button for this purpose.

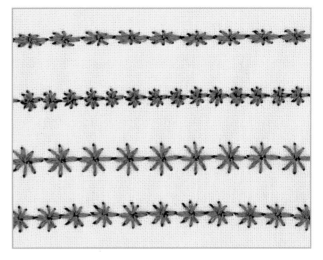
Altered asterisk

Altering or Changing Stitches

> *Note: All default settings are different on each machine. These examples are from the Baby Lock® Ellisimo® machine. Your stitches may not look exactly the same.*

Some stitches can be altered a multitude of ways. Some stitches cannot be altered at all and must be used at the default setting. Some can only be altered slightly. As you work with this technique you will become more familiar with how stitches can be changed. You will also have stitches you will use more than others. If the same stitch appears in different sections of your machine, chances are they can be altered in different ways.

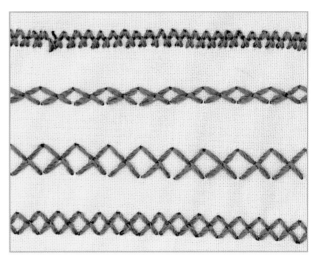
Cross-stitches

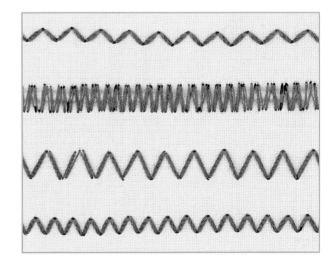
Rickrack

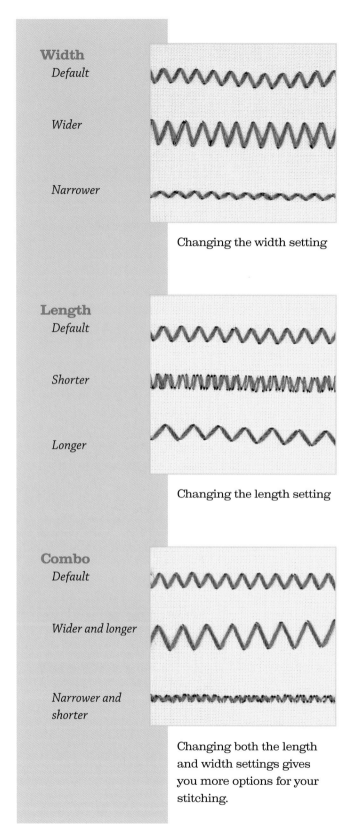

Width
Default

Wider

Narrower

Changing the width setting

Length
Default

Shorter

Longer

Changing the length setting

Combo
Default

Wider and longer

Narrower and shorter

Changing both the length and width settings gives you more options for your stitching.

STITCH LENGTH & WIDTH

The basics of changing the width

On most standard sewing machines, the built-in decorative stitches range from 5mm–9mm in width. Because of this your stitches might not be exactly like mine. The images I have provided were sewn on a machine with a maximum width of 7mm. There is no wrong way to do this process, so size does not matter.

Increasing the default setting will make the stitch wider.

Decreasing the default setting will make the stitch narrower.

The basics of changing the length

As a rule of thumb, the higher the number of the length setting, the looser (farther apart) the stitch will be. The lower the number, the denser the stitch will be. This is something you will have to explore for yourself. I will give you a basic formula for each project. You may need to adjust from there. You can always change the setting slightly up or down. If a single stitch pattern needs to be a specific length, for example, the length in inches is specified. I cannot tell you the exact setting for the length, because all the machines are different. So you will need to play with the length settings and sew the pattern out on the test sheet. You can then measure the length and adjust the setting if you need to. Remember nothing has to be an exact measurement. Getting it close is good enough.

Increasing the default setting will make the stitch longer.

Decreasing the default setting will make the stitch shorter.

THE BASICS OF MIRROR IMAGING

The mirror-image feature changes the orientation of a stitch from the default setting, up and down and/or left to right. Some stitches will not allow this change, some only up and down, and some only left to right. Check your manual. This is something that has to be played with to understand how the stitches change direction. When you alter this way, the stitch will sometimes stitch out upside down. The only way to know what it will look like is to test it first on a test sheet (see page 27). If your machine does not have the mirror-image feature, simply flip your fabric so the stitch will stitch out in the desired direction. This is where testing the stitch to see where it goes is a MUST.

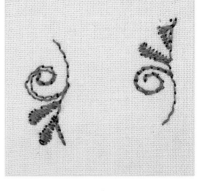

a. Mirroring vertically

Vertical mirror imaging =
FLIPPED UP OR DOWN/TOP TO BOTTOM

Reversing the vertical orientation of a stitch flips it from top to bottom. In most cases the top of the stitch image on the screen or in a figure on your machine is where the stitch will start and the bottom is where the stitch will end (a).

If you want to stitch out a single stitch pattern of a leaf, you may need to mirror the pattern so the stem or the bottom of the leaf will stitch out first (b).

b. Mirroring vertically

If you want the leaves on this stitch to appear to be growing up from the ground, flip it vertically (c).

I recommend stitching out a test before you stitch on your quilt; otherwise the stitch you want could be upside down.

c. Mirroring vertically

Horizontal mirror imaging =
FLIPPED RIGHT OR LEFT/SIDE TO SIDE

Reversing the horizontal orientation of the stitch flips it from side to side or left to right. In most cases the image on the screen will stitch out facing the direction shown below.

This stitch will have the straight edge facing right and the funky uneven edge facing left.

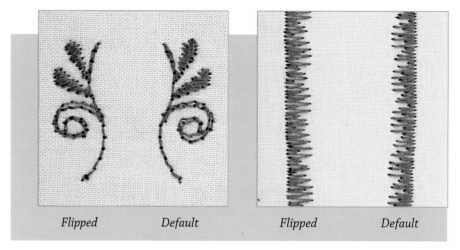

| *Flipped* | *Default* | *Flipped* | *Default* |

Mirroring horizontally   Mirroring horizontally

Combining horizontal and vertical mirror imaging =
FLIPPED UP AND DOWN AND SIDE TO SIDE

This is a perfect example of flipping the single stitch vertically, then flipping horizontally. On a few occasions the stitch can benefit from being altered this way.

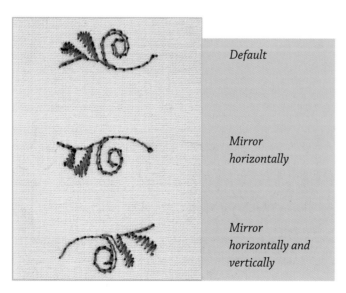

Default

Mirror horizontally

Mirror horizontally and vertically

Mirror both vertically and horizontally

Combining vertically and horizontally

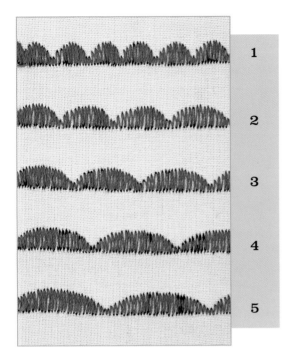

Elongation

Small or large stitches

Some stitches can only be selected as small or large. If that is the case and I tell you to use the maximum size width, then select the large stitch setting. If I tell you to make the stitch smaller (example: 4.0 width), then select the small stitch setting.

Elongation

Some of the newer machines have this feature. The elongation key is only for the satin stitches. You can choose from 5 automatic length settings. If you have this feature it is an easy way to make your satin stitches longer or shorter.

If your machine doesn't have this feature, simply adjust the stitch length manually to get the pattern as long as is specified and stitch over the pattern multiple times to get the density of stitching you desire.

Density

This is how solid the stitch is. It is more obvious in a satin stitch. When dense, the satin stitch will be solid with none of the background fabric showing through. When the satin stitch is looser, some of the background fabric shows through. The lower the length setting, the denser the stitch will be. If your machine does not have dense enough stitches to suit you, simply stitch over them one or two more times.

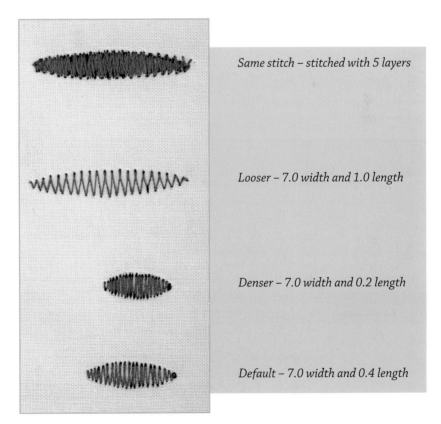

Same stitch – stitched with 5 layers

Looser – 7.0 width and 1.0 length

Denser – 7.0 width and 0.2 length

Default – 7.0 width and 0.4 length

Density

Tapering the stitch or stitching to a point

Some stitches will taper to a point automatically. This is very useful on the satin stitches. If you have this feature, it will be described in your manual. All the machines do this differently, so there is no standard format to tell you how to set up your machine. It is a great tool for drawing leaves and tree branches to a point.

Satin stitch made from zigzag 7.0 width and 0.2 length

Taper to a point by turning the fabric and pulling the stitch sideways to a point

Taper key/feature on machine

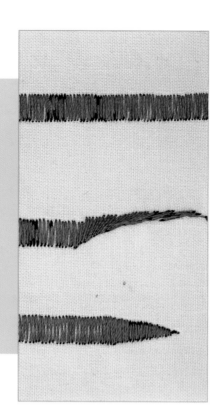

Tapering to a point

If your machine doesn't have this feature, you can still create a taper or point. Set your machine for a satin stitch. When you want the stitch to taper, just turn the fabric sideways and pull it to a point. It will take a little practice, but it is well worth the effort. Try it on a test sheet.

Turn fabric in a circle to spiral to the center

Turn fabric side to side

Normal stitching

Turn fabric side to side

Normal stitching

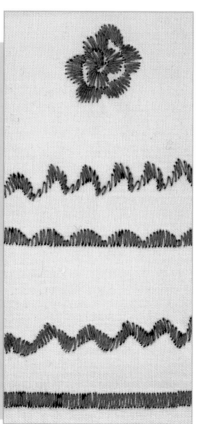

Distortion

TURNING THE FABRIC TO DISTORT

This is done just the way it sounds. By turning the fabric one way or the other you can alter or distort the stitch. You are doing the steering.

LOOSE STITCHES

Sometimes my machine will stitch out with loose stitches. If it decides to do that, I just go with it. Most of the time it will readjust itself, so I do not mind if this happens once in a while. If the machine continues to do this all the time, it is time to get it serviced. Something inside has slipped and a professional needs to adjust it.

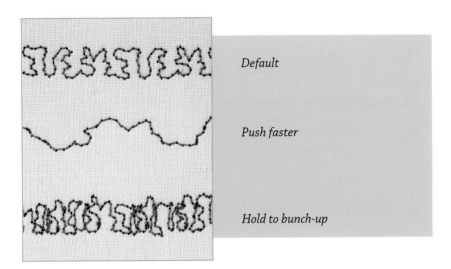

Default

Push faster

Hold to bunch-up

Pushing or holding the fabric

PUSH FASTER OR HOLD TO BUNCH UP

Simply push the fabric under the presser foot while stitching or hold the fabric so it will not feed, allowing the stitches to pile up on themselves. This is a very simple way to alter a stitch. I used this method all the time when I had my old vintage machine. We will use this technique in the scribbling exercise (page 28).

Allowing the Bobbin Thread to Show

By adjusting the bobbin tension you can control whether or not it shows on the top of your work. It is a fun way to add texture. You can alter the look of a stitch by adding a bright color bobbin thread and allowing it to show more on the surface of the quilt. It will create an outline on the edge of the stitch. I use only black poly thread and I allow it to show. I find that white bobbin thread dilutes the color of the top thread.

BOBBIN TENSION BASICS

Lower (loosen) the bobbin tension if you want the bobbin thread to show on the surface of your work.

If the bobbin thread is showing on the top and you don't want it to, raise (tighten) the bobbin tension until the thread doesn't show on the surface.

On decorative stitches with a lot of detail, lowering the bobbin tension can help prevent thread breakage. I recommend playing with this on a test sheet to achieve different looks. I always lower the tension when using metallic threads.

Turn the screw on the bobbin case to the right (clockwise) to tighten the bobbin thread tension. Turn the screw left (counterclockwise) to loosen the bobbin thread tension.

Couching

Couching involves stitching down a strand of yarn with a simple stitch. You can take this in a lot of directions by the stitch you select and the number of yarns you use. For example, we will be using a detailed decorative stitch with a bright color thread to stitch down a simple, solid color yarn on some of our background images. The Twisted/Gathered Yarn technique is one I developed using 3 colors of yarn all with different textures. They are twisted in one direction, then gathered and stitched down (page 31).

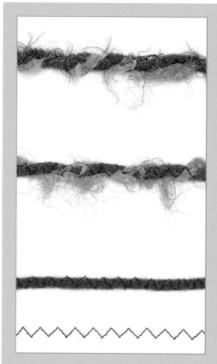

Couching using 3 yarns twisted as you sew

Couching using 2 yarns twisted as you sew

Couched yarn using 3-stitch zigzag stitch

3-stitch zigzag stitch – stitch used for all twisted/gathered yarn

The yarns used in this couching sample are chenille, eyelash yarn, and a ribbon yarn.

I recommend the three-stitch zigzag for this technique. It will be in the utility section on your machine. When set at 3.5 width and 1.0 length, this stitch will hold the yarn down securely and will also prevent slippage. The look of couching can be changed dramatically by adding decorative stitches instead of the simple zigzag or by stitching with contrasting thread.

Securing Threads

A single stitch pattern will tie off at the beginning and the end of the stitch. For the other stitches I do not tie off each thread. If I want the thread to hold on the back and not come loose, I flip the piece over and pull on the bobbin thread to bring a loop of the top thread to the back.

Using a large needle I grab the loop and pull the top thread to the back. If you give the top thread a tug it will hold better. This is usually enough to suit me. If it keeps popping to the top and making the stitch unravel, I dab the thread on the back with a tiny dot of stick glue.

Materials
FABRIC

When it comes to fabric I am an "everything but the kitchen sink" kind of person. I do have a basic rule on the foundation fabric. It is a smooth, high thread count fabric, either commercial or painted with my layered painted fabric technique (see Resources, page 94). I use cotton, rayon, or linen. The smooth fabric allows the decorative stitch threadwork to be more visible. If you use a loosely woven fabric, the detailed stitches can disappear. I put all this time into the machine work, so I do not want to have the detail work fade out on me.

I do however, use textured fabric, velvets, upholstery fabric, or old sweaters as accents for my ground and areas that are not the main focus. This is what I mean about "everything but the kitchen sink." I have collected fabrics for years. I will cut up old clothing if it is a particularly fabulous fabric and it is something I will not wear anymore.

For the projects in this book we will be using commercial fabrics that have solid color or small patterns. This way you can focus on the stitches and your work will not get lost in a fabric that has a bold pattern.

Fabric scraps

This process is perfect for those small bits of fabric that you have been collecting. I have bins of different sizes of scraps from larger quarter-yard pieces all the way down to small strips. I dig through them to find pieces to layer and stitch down.

Velvet or velveteen

I use a lot of velvet or velveteen. They have a sculptural quality. They also absorb the light more than other fabrics, creating a visual texture if placed next to a different fabric. I love the way the decorative stitches look on these surfaces. We will be using velvet and velveteen in some of our projects. You can add another layer of batting behind them and they will pop up even more.

BATTING

I use Fairfield Poly-fil Low-Loft® quilt batting for everything. The low loft provides enough puffy foundation so my work does not look flat. I can add more layers to areas if I want them to be thicker.

STABILIZER

I only have one major rule: Always use stabilizer. If I want puckering of my fabric I will create it under my control. Without stabilizer you will have allover uncontrolled puckering. I use a medium-weight tear-away stabilizer. I do not tear it away, but I can if I want to. Any medium-weight stabilizer will work, tear-away or cut-away. Just make sure it is not too thin. The stabilizer always goes on the back of the piece or the bottom, with the quilt batting in between. That way the piece is not too flat. If I am stitching an area that has dense machine work I will add another layer of stabilizer to that area for more support.

Always cut the stabilizer bigger than the batting and foundation fabric. Leave about 1" of stabilizer so you can run the stitches off the fabric onto the stabilizer. When you square off the piece you won't have to worry about the stitches being too short or not reaching the edge of the fabric.

On some projects with heavy stitching, I recommend using two sheets of stabilizer instead of just one. Simply layer the two sheets and treat them as one.

THREADS
30-wt. & 40-wt. threads

I use polyester or rayon threads most of the time. They are strong and colorful. Also, there is not too much lint from this thread. I like that feature for the thread. It puts less stress on your sewing machine. I usually choose 30- or 40- weight. Using a thick, bulky thread for the detailed decorative stitches may cause excessive breakage because of piercing the fabric more.

Variegated threads

This process is perfect for the variegated threads. There are all sorts of brands. My favorite is YLI Variations™ thread. It is a 35-wt. polyester. It is not too thick and not too thin. It can take stitching a very detailed stitch without breaking. There are about 20 wonderful bright colors and neutrals also. I buy the 1000 yard spools and they last a very long time. This thread adds great interest for leaves, stems, and shapes.

Thread breakage

If I have a lot of thread breakage, the first thing I check is to see if I have threaded the machine properly. If that is not the problem, I then lower the top thread tension. If the thread still continues to break I will then change the needle. If the thread continues to break, I will change the thread. Some days certain threads will give me more trouble than usual. I think this may have something to do with humidity and temperature change. I am all about stress-free sewing. If something is not working I move on to something else that does.

Adding Texture

I love texture! This whole process is about texture. If I want more texture in an area, I use bunched up tulle, onion bags (or any fruit or vegetable bags), ribbon, or paper. I find that anything that I can sew through that will not stress out my machine is fair game. Use your imagination and find what works for you.

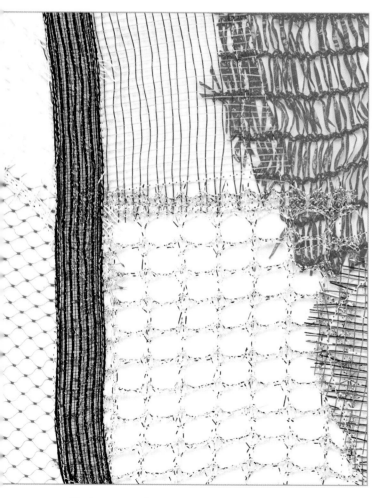

Texture samples

The sample picture on page 22 shows an orange bag, vintage silver scarf, vinyl woven floral accents in several colors, onion bag, and black metallic ribbon.

YARN

Try for three different textures of yarn for the best results. I use eyelash yarns and knobby yarns with my "Twisted/Gathered Yarn" technique (page 31). This is a perfect technique to use all those wonderful yarns you have been collecting. If you have not been collecting yarns, you will now. Just what you need—one more cool supply to collect! There is an abundance of colorful, soft, and textured yarn out there in the world. If you don't have any yarn stores locally, check for them online. One skein will last you a long time. That way you can buy one of everything you like. I have a bin in my studio filled with yarn. I just dig through and pull out what I like.

Yarn samples

Tools
SCISSORS

Any trim scissors will work fine as long as they are sharp. I prefer spring-loaded scissors for trimming. My hands do not get as tired.

BOBBINS

I buy pre-wound black bobbins by the gross. I hate to wind bobbins and this frees me up to spend my time sewing. Pre-wound bobbins are of 50- or 60-wt. thread and they are wound very tightly, so they have more thread and will last longer. You can find these pre-wound bobbins in smaller quantities at your local sewing center. The standard size for pre-wound bobbins is size L. Check in your manual for the correct size for your machine. If you are interested in buying by the gross, I buy mine from Thread Art (see Resources, page 94).

If you do not want to use pre-wound bobbins, I suggest you wind at least 10 bobbins in the color thread you desire. That way you do not have to stop your flow of creativity to wind a bobbin. You can just pop one in and go on your merry stitching way.

NEEDLES

A size 90/14 works for everything, although you can use a 75/11. Make sure the needle is sharp. I change my needle about every 8–10 hours of stitching. If I am sewing through very highly textured fabric I will change the needle more often. I use a metallic needle if I am having trouble with thread breakage on the metallics.

GLOVES

I use garden gloves with the rubber palms so I can grip the fabric to push it through faster. I cut off the fingers so my hands can breathe. The rubber palms grip the fabric so I do not strain my hands as much.

TEMPLATES

I use templates all the time. Precut templates in various shapes can be purchased at any craft store. We will be cutting circles and squares for the projects in this book. If you do not have a circle and square template in a variety of sizes, then you can make do with using found objects from around your house for the circles. The squares can be measured with a ruler.

IRON

I use an iron with a high-heat steam setting. When you have a quilt with concentrated areas of stitching, the fabric will warp or curl up. The high steam heat works very well at making my quilts flat. Always put a pressing cloth between the iron and the quilt to protect the threadwork.

CANNED AIR

I use canned air to keep the lint out of my machine. Every time I change the bobbin, I clean that area with canned air. I also clean the top thread area several times a day with the canned air. It helps my machine to run smoothly.

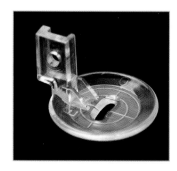

Echo quilting foot

Technical Stuff

Check your manual for specific instructions on these features:

PRESSER FOOT

Select a foot that allows good visibility. Any presser foot, metal or plastic, with a wide, clear opening will work just fine. You want to be able to see the beginning and the end of the stitch. I never change the presser foot to accommodate the stitches. This is part of the distorting process. Find a foot that works for you and you will not have to change it.

There are some machines that will not allow you to stitch out a selected decorative stitch unless you use the required foot. If this is the case you will need to follow your manual's directions and use the foot suggested.

I prefer an echo quilting foot. This foot comes as an attachment on a variety of machines. It is a large round clear plastic foot with edges that curve up. This foot is intended to be used for free-motion stitching. I have discovered that it works great with the feed dogs engaged.

Because the foot is clear, you can see everything you are doing. Because the foot is curled up on the edges, it glides over the textured surfaces and different thicknesses of fabric. The only drawback is when stitching satin stitches; the foot can sometimes get jammed up, because there is nothing pushing the fabric forward but you. Give it a little shove if this happens. If the stitches have bunched up and created a knot, stop and move up past the knot and start from there.

PRESSER FOOT UP

Most of the time I want the presser foot out of my way when I am done sewing. Some machines have a knee lift so you can raise the presser foot without having to let go of your work. On some machines the presser foot automatically lifts when you finish a sewing sequence. You can even set the amount of lift to different heights. I use the medium setting for everything.

NEEDLE UP & NEEDLE DOWN

Sometimes I want the needle to stay in the fabric when I end my sewing sequence. The advantage is that you will stay in the exact spot where you ended. Sometimes I want it to be up out of the fabric. You can set your machine to either option. Every machine I've had has this feature, even the older ones. It could be listed in your manual under needle placement or needle position. It is a very useful feature.

PIVOT FEATURE

The pivot feature is a combination of the preceding two features. When you stop sewing, the needle is down and the presser foot is up so you can pivot your work. When you start sewing again the presser foot will automatically lower. Most newer machines have a key function for this. You can also adjust the height of the presser foot. If your machine doesn't have this feature, you can manually combine the presser foot up and needle down features.

LOWERING THE FEED DOGS

If you lower the feed dogs on decorative stitches they will totally distort. This can be a wonderful effect, so I encourage you to experiment with this technique. I personally do not lower the feed dogs often. I will lower them to do the background stitching on the foundation fabric or while stitching some of the ground fabric or filler stitches. (See Preparing the foundation fabric, page 29, for more information.)

You can cover more area in a shorter period of time with the feed dogs down, but you have more control of the stitch with the feed dogs up.

> *Caution:* If you are using the maximum width for the stitch with the feed dogs lowered, the needle could slam into the side of the foot plate causing broken needles, damage to your machine, or harm to you from flying needles. The solution for this is ALWAYS keep the width 0.5 under the maximum width. For example, if your machine maximum width is 7.0, then select 6.5 and you will be safe. When project instructions say to select the maximum width minus 0.5, we will be lowering the feed dogs.

SPEED CONTROL

You can set the maximum speed on your machine. I keep my speed control in the middle, although if I want a more accurate stitch, I will lower my speed setting a bit more. If I want a very distorted stitch I set my speed to the maximum. Some machines will have a default setting for speed. This means you cannot sew too fast for certain stitches.

THREAD CUTTER

If you are lucky to have a thread cutter on your machine, use it. In this process there are a lot of threads to trim. Using your thread cutter will cut your thread-trimming time in half. If you notice that after using the thread cutter the upper thread is pulling out of the needle or the lower thread is not coming up to the surface, you

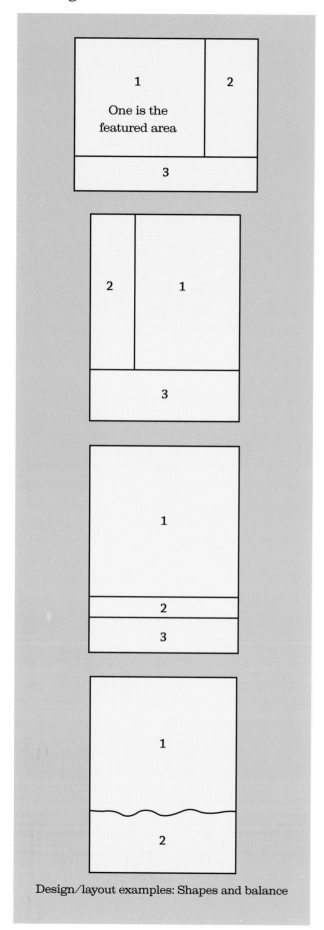

Design/layout examples: Shapes and balance

might need to have the cutting blade replaced. It is probably dull.

REBOOTING YOUR MACHINE

Sometimes, because of all the altering of the stitches, computerized machines will start to act funny. If you select a stitch and it is not stitching out like it is supposed to or if it's supposed to be wide and dense and it is stitching out thin and loose, your machine needs a reboot. Turn it off for about 20 seconds and then restart. That should clear everything and you will be good to go from there.

Design and Layout
ABSTRACT REALISM

I call the style of this work abstract realism. The abstract quality frees me up to go with any color or shape. I do not have to worry about perspective. The realism brings in familiar images.

WORKING SMALL

When I was in art school in the late 1970s, I was studying under M. Joan Lintault. One of the assignments was to create 6" by 6" fiber pieces made out of anything. This was a great exercise. I learned that when working small and fast, I would take more risks. When I started to explore this decorative stitch process, I worked the same way. The small size allowed me to be fearless when picking color combinations and stitches.

COLOR

Color, color, and more color. I love color. I totally trust my gut instinct when it comes to picking color for my quilts. Working on a small scale helped me to develop a stronger color sense. Sometimes I will have an idea of colors I want to combine and sometimes I just pick what is in front of me. Working abstractly allows me to combine colors not seen in nature.

SHAPE AND BALANCE

I like to create balance by working in twos or threes. I will have one area that is the main focus and other areas that add interest and connect all three areas together.

SIZE

It is very important to find a size that you are comfortable working in. This is a physical technique, turning and pushing in all directions. I have tried to work big but I am always miserable when I do. It's too hard on my body. My most comfortable size is 30" x 40". It's big enough to create some fun images, but not so big that it stresses my body.

REPETITION

I use combinations of repetition in all my work. I have always done this.

Creating Depth

Layering images is the best way to create depth. Start with the background stitching and work forward, letting the earlier stitches poke out from behind the later ones.

Inspiration

I get inspiration from everywhere—gardens at different times of the day, driving through the country, children's drawings, seed catalogs, books on art or geology, magazine ads, dreams, grid patterns—the sky's the limit! I always have a digital camera with me. Start looking at everything as a potential image for your quilt. Creating collage journals is another wonderful way to do rough drafts for quilt designs.

Practice, Practice, Practice

This process is like anything else—the more you work at it, the better you will get.

Beginning/Middle/Ending
ALWAYS USE A TEST SHEET

Make a test sheet with one sheet of stabilizer and one sheet of muslin. Practice your stitch to see if it is the correct size and that it is stitching out in the right direction. It is better to make a mistake on the test sheet rather than on the quilt. I have a drawer full of test sheets and use them as a reference tool.

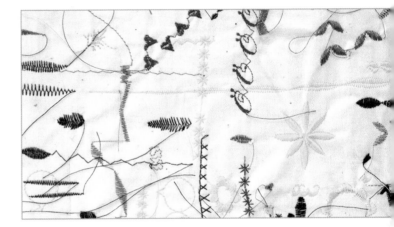
Test sheet

STITCH A SAMPLER

Introduce yourself to the stitches by making a sampler. You will also get a better feel for your machine. I do small samplers all the time. It is also a way to get a sewing fix if you are in between projects. I keep my stitch samplers in a drawer and pull them out for reference on the stitches. They can be made more decorative or they can be simple, but either way, they're a great reference tool. Use a permanent fine-point marker to note the size and number of each stitch on the fabric. The cover photo is a decorative sampler I made.

SCRIBBLING EXERCISE

The scribbling exercise is a great way to loosen you up. It will help you to understand how easy it is to alter the stitches by your movements. It is not intended to be a finished piece. Stitch in big circles, zigzags or loops. Let it be sloppy.

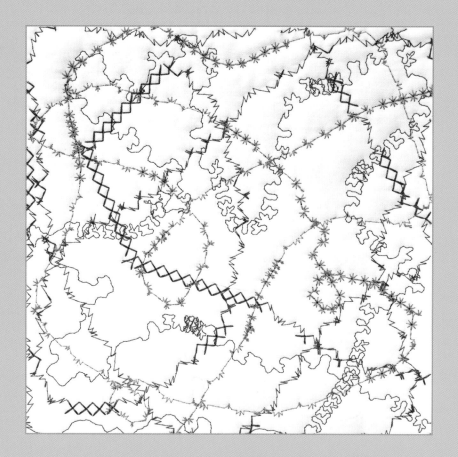

Materials:

11" x 11" medium-weight
 stabilizer
9" x 9" low-loft batting
9" x 9" muslin
Rayon or poly thread in
 red, blue, and green

Foundation Fabric

Sandwich = stabilizer + batting
 + muslin

Red scribbling

* Thread the machine with red thread.
* Select cross-stitch, Max width & Max length.
* Start stitching out normally.
* Now push the fabric faster.
* Turn the fabric from side-to-side.
* Hold the fabric to bunch up the stitch.
* Turn in circles.
* Do loops and zigzags.

By now you should be getting the idea of this exercise. This is the easiest way to alter the stitch.

Green scribbling

* Thread the machine with green thread.
* Select asterisk stitch, Max width & Max length.
* Repeat as in red scribbling.

Blue scribbling

* Thread the machine with blue thread.
* Select stipple stitch, default setting.
* Repeat as in red scribbling.

* Add another color thread and pick a stitch of your own if you desire to work more on this exercise

BACKGROUND/FOUNDATION FABRIC

This is a wholecloth process. Picking the right background fabric is important to the overall design. The entire quilt will be built from this foundation. When you are just learning this process, choose a background fabric that is solid or has small patterns and contrasting fabrics for other areas. With careful fabric selection, you can concentrate on the stitch patterns and not have to worry about the fabric overwhelming the piece. Work your way up to bolder backgrounds or hand-painted fabrics.

Preparing the foundation fabric

Make a sandwich by layering the stabilizer (one or two sheets as called for in the projects), batting, and background fabric. Place the batting and foundation fabric in the center of the stabilizer so it frames the batting and fabric.

Select a thread of a similar color to the fabric to create a soft, almost invisible background texture, or use a contrasting thread color to create a visible background texture. I like to work in a grid on the background.

Prepare the foundation by machine quilting the three main layers. The machine quilting holds them together and provides background texture. You could use any of the stitches in your machine for this, but I have provided you several of my favorites.

Stitching the background

Thread the machine with desired thread color and select a background stitch. Do not worry about the lines being straight. It is OK if they are not perfect. Stitch with the feed dogs up or down. Remember, if the feed dogs are down, you will need to push the fabric (see the examples on page 30).

* Start in a top corner and stitch to the opposite corner.

* Repeat every inch. Don't measure, just estimate the distance.

* Repeat, starting in the opposite top corner to create a grid pattern.

* Now your foundation fabric is ready for the next step in your project.

Place fabric & batting in center of stabilizer.

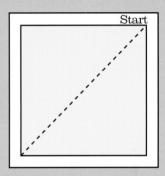

Starting in top right corner, stitch to opposite corner.

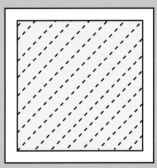

Sew a row every inch, covering the entire fabric surface.

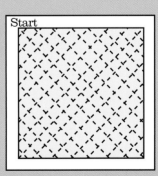

Starting in the left top corner, stitch to opposite corner. Repeat every inch to cover fabric surface.

SUGGESTED STITCHES FOR BACKGROUND

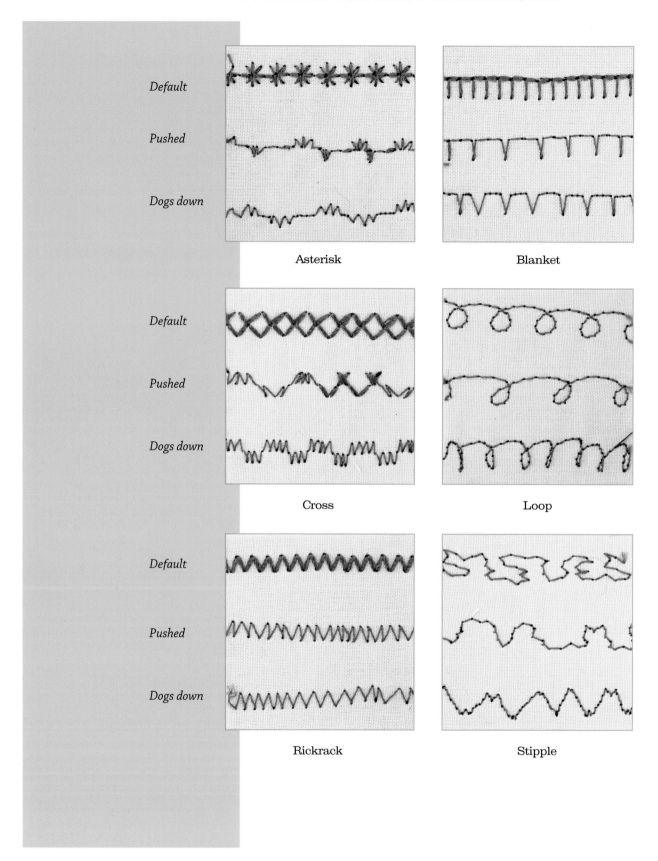

Default

Pushed

Dogs down

Asterisk

Blanket

Cross

Loop

Rickrack

Stipple

TWISTED/GATHERED YARN

Couching three strands of twisted and gathered yarn along the edge finishes the quilt. I also use this technique to separate the ground from the plants or to stitch around the border. It is great for camouflage, covering up mistakes! Use your imagination.

> *Note: Set the machine pivot feature or for needle down and presser foot up. Each time you stop sewing the needle will be down and the foot will raise. This will hold the fabric and allow you to slide the yarn under the foot. If your machine does not have this feature, you can lift the foot manually. Just make sure the needle is down so the fabric does not slip.*

Select a three-stitch zigzag stitch, 3.5 width & 1.0 length.

Take the 3 strands of yarn and stitch them down on the edge of your art quilt at ground level.

Twist the yarns in one direction and using a pushing tool, push a loop of the twisted yarn under the foot and stitch it down. Practice on a test sheet first.

Repeat across the top of the ground all the way to the other side. Make sure the yarn is twisted in one direction as you sew. You can make small loops or large loops. The more you do this technique, the better control you will have.

Large loop – 3 yarn – twisted/ gathered yarn technique

Small loop – 3 yarn – twisted/ gathered yarn technique

Couching 3 yarns, twisted then gathered into small loops as you sew.

CROPPING THE QUILT

After preparing the foundation, square off the edges of the quilt with a marker. This is the line or the edge to crop the quilt when it is finished. It helps to see the exact size you are working with and keep from wasting time working on an area that will be cut away.

When you crop or square off a quilt, some of the stitches will be cut off. Do not worry about the stitches coming out. Sewing on a binding or couching yarn along the edges will hold the stitches in place.

FINISHING THE QUILT

Serging the back to the front

No matter how large my quilt is, I use a wholecloth fabric on the back and serge it to the front.

Cut the backing 1" larger around the whole quilt. Smooth this as flat as possible and pin it in place. Serge the back to the front, trimming the extra fabric off as you go. You do not need to quilt the back to the front. The piece is ready for any form of binding and adding a sleeve that you desire.

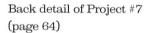

Framing

If you choose to display your quilt matted and in a frame under glass, there is no need to finish the back or the edges. The finished piece needs to be at least ½" larger than the opening of the mat so the mat sits on top of the quilt and the edges do not show.

Back detail of Project #7
(page 64)

Hanging with a dowel rod

Hang quilts 15" or smaller that are not framed with a ¼" dowel rod. Measure the dowel 2" wider than the quilt. Use a small hand saw to cut it to size and sand the ends smooth with a sanding block. Color the dowel black with an extra-wide flat tip permanent black marker. The ¼" dowels come in 36"–48" lengths. The dowel rods, hand saw, and sanding blocks can be found at your local hardware store.

How to Use These Projects

There are 14 projects in all, designed to be done in sequence. Each of the small projects introduces new techniques and design ideas. The techniques presented in projects #1–#6 are combined in GARDEN PARTY, which refers back to each project for design and technique information. The techniques presented in projects #7–#12 are combined in FOREST FROLIC.

I have selected the color scheme for each project in this book. You are welcome to use my colors of fabric, thread and yarn, or you can alter the colors as you wish.

In most cases, once the machine is threaded with a particular color, several steps in different places in the project will be done. This is to keep threading and rethreading your machine to a minimum.

The stitches we will use for the projects are pictured on page 11.

Keep a test sheet (page 27) handy to experiment with stitch settings before stitching on your project.

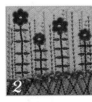

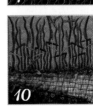

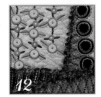

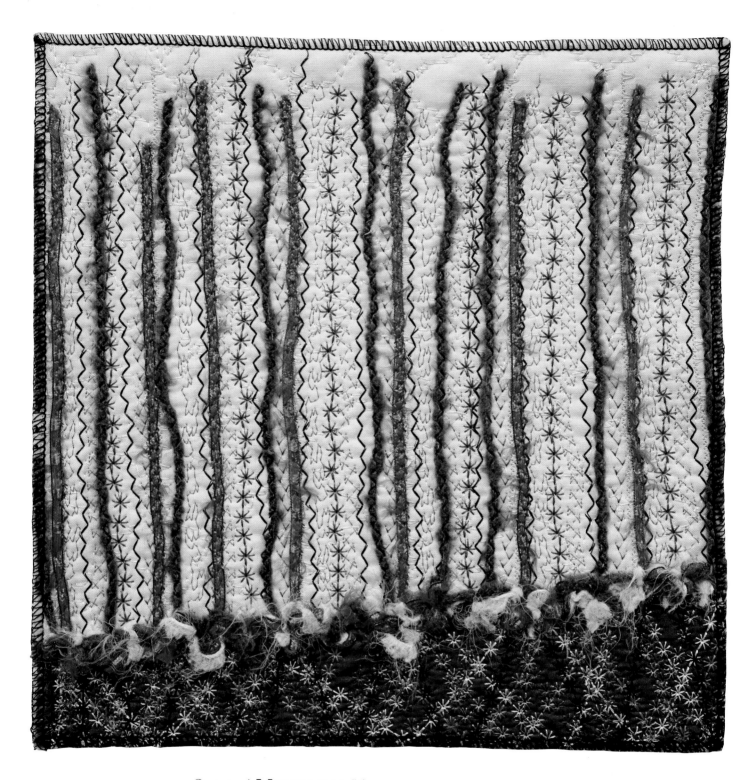

Project #1 MARSHLAND #1, 10½" x 10½", made by the author

Project #1 MARSHLAND #1

When I first started to use the stitches to paint landscapes, I began with a marshland format. This layout is the foundation for all my fantasy gardens. This project focuses on the utility stitches. It demonstrates that any stitch can be used to create surface design, although you are welcome to use different stitches if you desire. The idea is to make layered rows of plant forms.

Materials

12" x 12" medium-weight stabilizer
11" x 11" low-loft batting
11" x 11" solid yellow—foundation
3" x 11" dark green fabric—ground

Threads
Dark green
Gold
Light green
Medium green
Orange
Rust
Yellow

Stitches
Asterisk
Blind hem
Cross
Faggot
Feather
Rickrack
Stipple

Yarns
Dark green
Orange
Yellow

Foundation

Thread the machine with yellow thread and prepare the foundation fabric (page 29) using the cross-stitch.

Ground

Cut the dark green fabric in a curvy line from the upper right corner to the opposite side as shown. Pin it to the bottom of the foundation fabric. The decorative stitches will hold it in place.

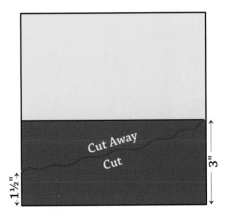

Cut and place the ground fabric on the foundation.

If your machine has the pivot feature, use it while stitching a "W" pattern across the ground. When you stop at the bottom of the ground, the needle should be down and the presser foot will rise automatically so you can pivot your fabric and stitch back to the top edge of the ground.

Thread Color	Stitch Selection	Ground
all thread colors	asterisk stitch, Max width & Max length	Each time you load a new thread color, stitch a "W" pattern across the dark-green ground, offsetting the stitching each time.

GROUND STITCH PLACEMENT

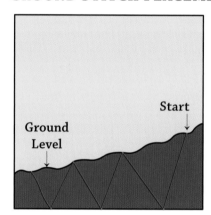

Pivot to stitch a "W" pattern on the ground.

For each color of thread you use creating the marsh plants on the foundation, you will be adding a layer of stitches in that same color to the ground, creating color balance.

Otherwise, simply stop with the needle down, raise the presser foot manually, and pivot the fabric before proceeding.

MARSH PLANTS PLACEMENT

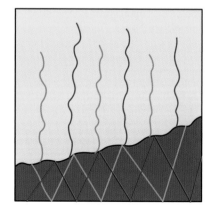

Offset each addition of ground stitching.

Add the marsh plants as follows:

Thread Color	Stitch Selection	Marsh Plants
gold	faggoting cross-stitch, 5.0 width & Max length	Starting at the edge of the ground, stitch 6 curvy lines on the foundation, stopping at different heights. These lines are intended to be plants, so they do not need to be evenly spaced.
orange	stipple stitch, 5.0 width & Max length	Stitch 7 curvy lines, stopping at different heights.
light green	blind hem stitch, Max width & 1.0 length	Stitch 6 curvy lines, stopping at different heights.
rust	asterisk stitch, Max width & Max length	Stitch 6 curvy lines, stopping at different heights.
medium green	feather stitch, 5.0 width & Max length	Stitch 6 curvy lines, stopping at different heights.
dark green	rickrack stitch, 2.5 width & Max length	Stitch 12 curvy lines, stopping at different heights. Couch 9 curvy lines using the fuzzy green yarn, stopping at different heights.
rust	cross-stitch, 4.0 width & 2.5 length	Couch 8 curvy lines using the orange ribbon yarn, stopping at different heights.

Twisted/Gathered Yarn Technique

Couch green, orange, and yellow yarn along the edge of the ground (page 31).

When couching the yarns, I do not use a couching foot because this does not need to be perfect. If you miss some of the yarn the first time, you can always stitch over it a second time.

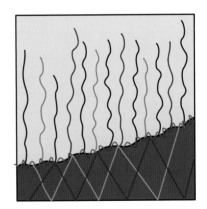

Couch gathered/twisted yarn along the ground.

Finishing

Finish as desired (page 32).

Project #2 MARSHLAND #2, 10½" x 10½", made by the author

Project #2 MARSHLAND #2

We will use decorative stitches to create this marshland landscape and add a simple flower made from fabric and outline stitches.

Materials

12" x 12" medium-weight stabilizer

11" x 11" low-loft batting

11" x 11" solid peach—foundation

3" x 11" orange—ground

3" x 6" red—flowers

    Cut 2 large flowers and 2 small flowers using the templates provided (page 41).

Threads

Brown

Dark green

Orange

Peach

Red

Variegated medium
   green

Yellow/gold

Stitches

Asterisk

Chicken foot

Cross

Hollow checker

Petal

Rickrack

Scallop

Solid leaf

Solid leaf with stem

Yarns

Orange

Red

Yellow

Note: *If you do not have the elongation feature, experiment with your test sheet to achieve the length specified.*

If you do not have the single stitch pattern feature, sew the flower center slowly and stop stitching when the pattern is complete. Leave the needle down and pivot the fabric so you can stitch over the pattern a second (or even third) time to achieve the density you want.

Foundation

Thread the machine with peach thread and prepare the foundation fabric (page 29) using the cross-stitch.

Ground

Cut the orange fabric in a curvy line from the upper-right corner to the opposite side as you did in project #1 (page 35). Pin it to the bottom of the foundation fabric.

Thread Color	Stitch Selection	Ground
all thread colors	asterisk stitch, Max width & Max length	Each time you load a new thread color, stitch a "W" pattern across the dark-green ground, offsetting the stitching each time as in Project #1.

Add the marsh plant and flower stitching as follows:

Thread Color	Stitch Selection	Marsh Plants & Flowers
yellow/ gold	hollow checker stitch, Max width & Max length	Starting at the edge of the ground, stitch 9 lines across the foundation, stopping at different heights, as in Project #1.
brown	chicken foot, Max width & 4.0 length	Stitch 9 lines, stopping at different heights.
red	asterisk stitch, Max width & Max length	Stitch 4 lines, stopping at different heights.
orange	scallop stitch, Max width & 0.3 length, elongation 1 (about ¼" long)	Stitch 4 lines, stopping at different heights.
variegated medium green	leaf with stem stitch, Max width & Max length	Stitch 5 lines, stopping at different heights. Mirror the stitch or turn the fabric so the leaves are pointing up.

Red flower placement

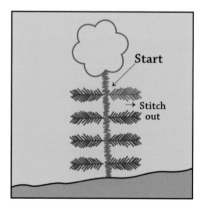

Adding the leaves

Thread Color	Stitch Selection	Marsh Plants & Flowers
dark green	stem stitch, Max width & 0.3 length	Pin the 4 red flowers in place and stitch 4 curvy stem lines.
	leaf stitch, Max width & Max length, single pattern	Stitch the leaves straight out from the stem. Try on a test sheet first. You may need to flip vertically with the mirror image tool or change the position of the fabric.
yellow/gold	rickrack stitch, 2.5 width & 1.0 length	Stitch around the edge of the flowers. Don't worry if some of the raw edges show. Let them be funky.
	petal stitch, Max width & 0.3 length, single pattern setting, elongation 1 (about ¼" long)	Stitch a wide, dense, oblong oval positioned horizontally in the center of each flower. Stitch multiple times to achieve good density.
red	rickrack stitch, 3.0 width & 1.0 length	Stitch a second layer around the edges of the flowers. The same stitch in different sizes and colors creates interest.
	grass stitch, Max width & 0.4 length	Stitch around the flower center with the flat edge of the stitch next to the yellow center as shown.

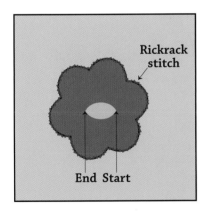

Stitching the flower center

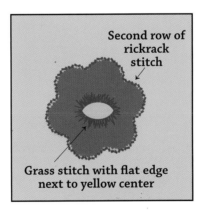

Flower details

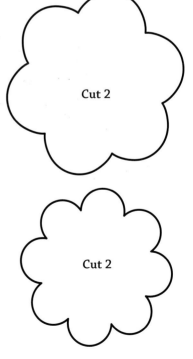

Flower templates

Twisted/Gathered Yarn Technique

Couch red, orange, and yellow yarn along the edge of the ground (page 31).

Finishing

Finish as desired (page 32).

Project #3 SPIKE FLOWER #1, 10½" x 10½", made by the author

Project #3 SPIKE FLOWER #1

In this project layers of surface design are created by stitching on top of cut fabric shapes.

Materials

12" x 12" medium-weight stabilizer

11" x 11" low-loft batting

11" x 11" light-orange check—foundation

3" x 11" orange/red—ground

4" x 12" medium/dark blue
Cut 3 squares 3½" x 3½"

3" x 3" orange/red fake suede
Cut 1 circle 2½" in diameter.

4" x 4" small dark green print
Cut 6 leaves with the template provided (page 45).

Threads

Cranberry red

Dark green

Variegated ocean
blue

Variegated peach

Stitches

Asterisk

Grass

Hollow flower

Loop

Petal

Scallop

Stem

Yarns

Blue

Green

Red

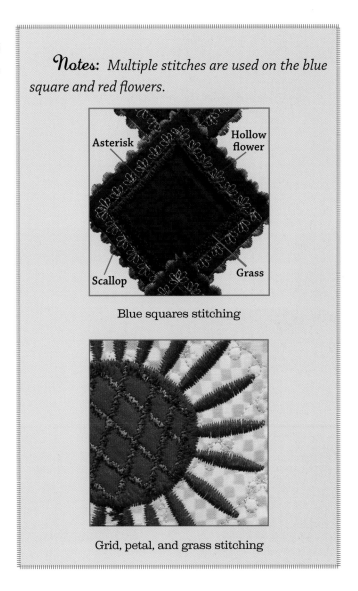

Notes: *Multiple stitches are used on the blue square and red flowers.*

Asterisk · Hollow flower · Scallop · Grass

Blue squares stitching

Grid, petal, and grass stitching

Foundation

Thread the machine with peach thread and prepare the foundation fabric (page 29) using the loop stitch, Max width & Max length.

Place the 3 blue squares as shown.

Blue squares and hollow stitch placement

Thread Color	Stitch Selection	Flowers, Leaves, and Blue Squares
peach	any hollow flower stitch any size	Stitch around the 3 squares ½" from the edges

Ground

Cut and position the orange/red fabric as shown and pin it to the bottom of the foundation fabric.

Ground fabric placement

Thread Color	Stitch Selection	Ground
all thread colors	asterisk stitch, Max width & Max length	Each time you load a new thread color, stitch a "W" pattern across the ground, offsetting the stitching each time as in Project #1.

Add the flower stitching as follows:

Thread Color	Stitch Selection	Flowers, Leaves, and Blue Squares
variegated ocean blue	stem stitch, 3.5 width & 0.4 length	Pin the 2½" red circle 2" from the right edge and 5" above the edge of the ground. Stitch lines ½" apart across the circle, creating a grid, see photo page 43.
	scallop stitch, Max width & 0.4 length, elongation 1 (about ¼" long)	Stitch around the edges of the top blue square with the curve of the scallop stitch facing out. You may need to turn the fabric or mirror this stitch. Repeat on the middle square, overlapping the scallop stitches on the top square. Repeat on the bottom square, starting and ending at the ground, see photo page 43.
dark green	stem stitch, Max width & 0.4 length	Stitch a fairly straight line from the red flower to the ground. Add a second row of stitches over the first line, turning the fabric to create a curvy line.
	grass stitch, 3.5 width & 0.4 length	Pin the 6 leaves in pairs along the stem about 1¼" apart. Stitch along the edges of the leaves with the uneven edge of the stitch facing out. Add a line of grass stitches to the blue squares with the flat edge against the hollow flower stitches.
cranberry red	petal stitch, Max width & 1.25" length, single pattern setting	Use your test sheet first to make sure you're happy with the size. Stitch a single petal, pivot, and stitch back over the petal. Repeat at ¼" intervals around the flower.
	grass stitch, Max width & 0.4 length	Stitch around the edge of the flower center with the uneven edge facing in.
	asterisk stitch, Max width & Max length	Add a row of stitches to the blue squares between the hollow flower and grass stitches.

Twisted/Gathered Yarn Technique

Couch red, blue, and green yarn along the edge of the ground (page 31).

Finishing

Finish as desired (page 32).

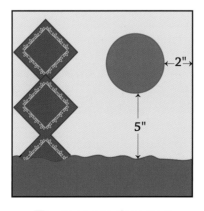

Flower center placement

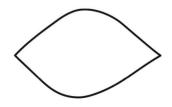

Leaf template

Project #4 SPIKE FLOWER #2, 10½" x 10½", made by the author

Project #4 SPIKE FLOWER #2

This is another simple flower with a fabric center. A repeated pattern of stitches is used on the ground while the same stitch is used for both the flower petals and the leaves.

Materials

    2 squares 12" x 12" medium-weight stabilizer

11" x 11" low-loft batting

11" x 11" bright green—foundation

4" x 11" violet/purple—ground

    Cut a curvy edge on one side for the ground.

4" x 4" purple with blue print

    Cut 1 circle 2" in diameter and 2 circles 1" in diameter for the flower centers.

Threads	**Stitches**
Kelly green	Asterisk
Mint green	Crescent
Orange	Detail feather
Variegated purple	Feather leaf
Violet	Grass
	Petal
	Rickrack
	Solid leaf with stem
Yarns	Stipple
Green	Zigzag
Orange	
Violet	

Foundation Fabric

Thread the machine with mint green thread and prepare the foundation fabric with 2 squares of stabilizer (page 29) using the stipple stitch, Max width minus 0.5, with the feed dogs dropped, which gives you control over the length. Let the stitch distort as you move the fabric. Be sure to raise the feed dogs when you finish the foundation preparation.

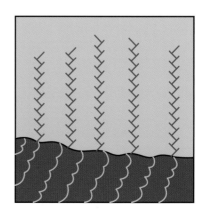

Crescent and feather stitch and ground placement

Add the flower and ground cover stitching as follows:

Thread Color	Stitch Selection	Background Plants, Flowers & Leaves	Ground
mint green	crescent stitch, Max width & 0.4 length, elongation 3 (about ½" long)		Stitch diagonal rows across the ground spaced 1" apart.
violet	feather stitch, Max width & Max length	Stitch 5 rows spaced about 2" apart, ending at different heights.	
	rickrack stitch, 2.0 width & 1.0 length	Pin the 1" fabric circles 3½" above the ground and the 2" circle 4" above the ground as shown on page 49. Stitch around the edges of the circles.	
Kelly green	zigzag stitch, 4.0 width & 0.2 length	Stitch curvy stems between the flowers and the ground.	
	petal stitch, Max width & 0.5 length, single pattern setting, elongation 5 (about 1½" long)	Test the stitch. It should be 1½" long. Stitch a leaf out from the stem; pivot and stitch back over the leaf. Stitch 2 pairs of leaves on each stem.	
variegated purple	petal stitch, Max width & 0.5 length, single pattern setting, elongation 4 (about 1" long)	Stitch a petal out from the center flower; pivot and stitch back over the petal. Repeat every ¼" around the center. Reset the stitch length to ¾" and stitch petals around the smaller flower centers. Press flat using a pressing cloth.	
	asterisk stitch, Max width & Max length		Stitch a row to the left of each row of crescent stitches.
orange	grass stitch, Max width & 0.3 length	Stitch 2 rows of grass stitch around the flower circles with the flat edges of the stitching back-to-back as shown on page 49. You'll need to mirror the stitch or turn the fabric for the uneven edges to point in opposite directions.	
	solid leaf with stem stitch Max width & 0.3 length	Stitch 9 rows of different heights. Make sure the leaves are pointing up.	
	feather leaf, Max width & 0.4 length		Stitch a row between the asterisk and crescent stitches.

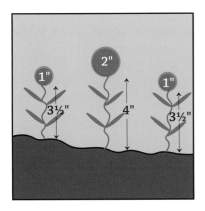

Flower placement

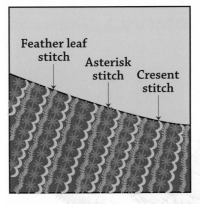

Ground stitching placement

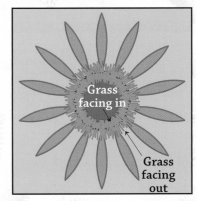

Petal and grass stitch placement

Twisted/Gathered Yarn Technique

Couch violet, orange, and green yarn along the edge of the ground (page 31).

Finishing

Finish as desired (page 32).

Project #5 SCALLOP FLOWER, 10½" x 10½", made by the author

Project #5 SCALLOP FLOWER

This project features a very simple flower done with a spiral technique and satin stitch that starts on the outside and spirals in. We'll use two sheets of stabilizer because the dense stitching will cause major warping of the quilt if we don't.

Materials

    2 squares 12" x 12" medium-weight stabilizer
    11" x 11" low-loft batting
    11" x 11" light teal with pink and teal pattern—foundation
    4" x 11" dark teal with small black print—ground

Threads

Dark teal
Hot pink
Seafoam green
Variegated
    burgundy
Variegated light
    pink

Stitches

Asterisk
Hollow leaf with
    stem
Petal
Punchwork
Satin zigzag
Scallop
Solid leaf with stem
Stipple

Yarns

Burgundy
Hot pink
Medium teal

Foundation Fabric

Thread the machine with variegated light pink thread and prepare the foundation fabric with 2 squares of stabilizer (page 29) using the stipple stitch, Max width minus 0.5, with the feed dogs dropped, which gives you control over the length. Let the stitch distort as you move the fabric. Be sure to raise the feed dogs when you finish preparing the foundation.

Cut and place the ground fabric at the bottom of the foundation and draw 5 circles as shown.

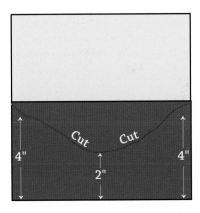

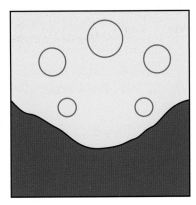

Ground fabric and flower circle placement

Add the flower and ground cover stitching as follows:

Thread Color	Stitch Selection	Background Plants, Flowers & Leaves	Ground
variegated light pink	stipple stitch, Max width & 1.0 length		Stitch 3 horizontal rows across the ground spaced 1" apart.
hot pink	punch work stitch, Max width & Max length	Stitch 6 rows ending at different heights as in Project #1.	
	scallop stitch, Max width & 0.3 length, elongation 5 (about ½" long)		Stitch a row above and below each row of stipple stitches.
seafoam green	hollow leaf with stem stitch, Max width & Max length	Stitch 7 rows of background plants ending at different heights. Mirror the stitch or turn the fabric so the leaves are pointing up.	
	asterisk stitch, Max width & Max length		Stitch 3 rows between the rows of hot pink scallop stitches.
dark teal	satin zigzag stitch, Max width & 0.3 length, elongation 1 (about ¼" long)	Stitch a stem from the 3" circle to the ground, then add stems to the other circles coming off the main stem. Stitch back over the stems, offsetting the stitch. You may want to mirror this stitch.	
	petal stitch, Max width & 0.5 length, elongation 5 (about 1" long)	Test that your stitch is 1" long. Stitch out from the stem, turning your fabric to curve at the end. Pivot and stitch a second layer back to the stem. Add 2 leaves per stem.	
variegated burgundy	scallop stitch, Max width & 0.3 length, elongation 1 (about ¼" long)	Stitch around the outside edge of a flower circle, then spiral in toward the center, overlapping the straight edge of the previous round of stitches. The scalloped edge of the stitch should face out. Repeat for all 5 flowers. You may need to press the quilt to flatten out flowers.	
	asterisk stitch, Max width & Max length		Stitch a row over the stipple stitching (between the rows of scallop stitches).
seafoam green	solid leaf with stem stitch, Max width & 0.3 length	Stitch 11 rows of background plants at different heights. Mirror the stitch or turn the fabric so the leaves are pointing up as in Project #4. It's OK to overlap the main flower and stem.	

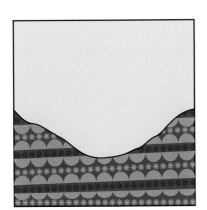

Scallop and asterisk
stitch placement

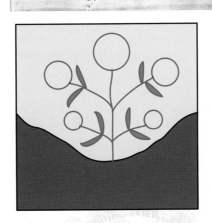

Stem placement

Scallop stitches spiraling in

Twisted/Gathered Yarn Technique

Couch medium teal, hot pink, and burgundy yarn along the edge of the ground (page 31).

Finishing

Finish as desired (page 32).

Project #6 SUNFLOWER #1, 10½" x 10½", made by the author

Project #6 SUNFLOWER #1

The sunflower features a woven grid pattern of stitching. This easy flower is versatile and can be made any size from very small to very large. I allowed the black bobbin thread to show on the background stitching by raising the top thread tension. Test to see if this is a look that you like.

Materials

12" x 12" medium-weight stabilizer
11" x 11" low-loft batting
11" x 11" light gold with a gold metallic pattern—foundation
4" x 11" dark gold
Cut 1 circle 2½" in diameter and 2 circles 1½" in diameter.
4" x 5" brown velveteen—ground
3" x 6" brown with white dots—ground

Threads

Dark green
Gold metallic
Gold (non-metallic)
Rust
Variegated brown

Yarns

Brown
Rust/orange
Yellow/gold

Stitches

Asterisk
Grass
Hollow leaf with stem
Satin diamond
Scallop
Solid leaf
Solid leaf with stem

Foundation

Thread the machine with non-metallic gold thread and prepare the foundation fabric (page 29) using the asterisk stitch, Max width minus .05 and drop the feed dogs, which gives you control over the length. Raise the top thread tension if you want the bobbin thread to show on top. Be sure to raise the feed dogs and readjust the tension when you finish preparing the foundation.

Ground

Cut the brown dot and velveteen ground fabrics as shown and pin them at the bottom of the foundation, overlapping the dot fabric with the velveteen.

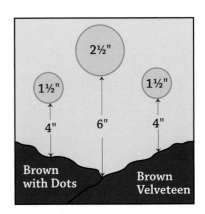

Ground and flower circle placement

Add the marsh plant, flowers, and ground cover stitching as follows:

Thread Color	Stitch Selection	Marsh Plants & Sunflowers	Ground
gold metallic	stem stitch, Max width & 0.3 length		Stitch a grid pattern on each of the ground fabrics, angling them slightly differently.
variegated brown	asterisk stitch, 4.0 width & 2.0 length	Position the flower centers as shown. Stitch a ¼" grid pattern on all 3 circles.	
dark green	diamond satin stitch, Max width & 0.3 length, elongation 3 (about ½" long)	Stitch stems on the three flowers.	
	feather leaf stitch, Max width & 1" long, single pattern setting	Stitch pairs of leaves where the points of each stem's diamond stitches meet, slowly turning the fabric so the leaves curl up at the end. Mirror the stitch or turn the fabric to make sure the base of the leaf starts at the stem.	
rust	scallop stitch, Max width & 0.3 length, elongation 1 (about ¼" long)	Start at the stem and stitch around the edge of the flower centers with the flat edge of the stitch against the fabric and the scallop edge facing out.	
	hollow leaf with stem stitch, Max width & Max length	Stitch 6 rows of background plants at different heights. Mirror the stitch or turn the fabric so the leaves point up.	
	solid leaf stitch with stem, Max width & 0.3 length	Stitch 12 rows of background plants at different heights. Mirror the stitch or turn the fabric so the leaves point up.	
	asterisk stitch, Max width & 0.3 length		Stitch a grid pattern over the stem stitch grid, offsetting the position of the lines.
gold metallic	grass stitch, Max width & 0.3 length	Stitch around each flower twice, inside the scallop stitches, with the uneven edge of the grass stitch facing in.	

Leaf placement

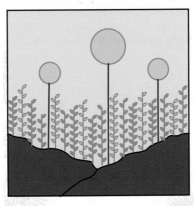

6 rows of hollow leaf stitch and
12 rows of solid leaf stitch

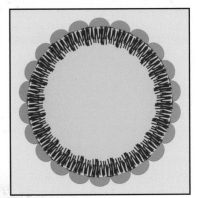

Grass stitch placement

Twisted/Gathered Yarn Technique

Couch yellow/gold, rust/orange, and brown yarn along the edge of the ground (page 31).

Finishing

Finish as desired (page 32).

GARDEN PARTY, 19" x 19", made by the author

GARDEN PARTY

This is a fun project that combines the techniques introduced in the first six projects. We will refer back to each project for design and techniques.

Materials

2 squares 21" x 21" medium-weight stabilizer
19" x 19" low-loft batting
19" x 19" solid seafoam green—foundation fabric
7" x 18" brown satin—ground and 4 squares 2½" x 2½"
2½" x 24" medium brown with gold—ground and flowers
6" x 15" teal with small pattern—ground and flowers
2" x 7" medium green—leaves

Stitches

Asterisk
Crescent
Diamond satin
Grass
Hollow leaf with stem
Petal
Punch work
Rickrack
Satin zigzag
Solid leaf
Solid leaf with stem
Stem
Stipple

Threads

Bronze
Dark green
Dark orange
Dark teal
Gold metallic with black
Orange
Seafoam green
Variegated brown
Variegated forest green
Variegated peach

Yarns

Brown
Dark teal
Medium brown
Orange

Foundation

Thread the machine with seafoam green thread and prepare the foundation fabric (page 29) using the stipple stitch, Max width minus .05 with the feed dogs dropped, which gives you control over the length. Raise the feed dogs when finished.

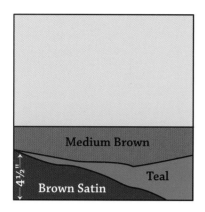

Ground

Ground

Place the top edge of the medium brown with gold fabric 7" from the bottom of the foundation fabric. Cut pieces of teal and brown satin and position as shown.

Thread the machine with bronze thread and using the same stipple stitch and settings, stitch diagonal rows across the ground 1" apart. Raise the feed dogs when finished.

Add the marsh plant, flowers, and ground cover stitching as follows:

Thread Color	Stitch Selection	Background Plants	Ground
all project thread colors	asterisk stitch, Max width & Max length		Stitch layers in a "W" pattern over the teal ground (Project #1, page 36).
dark teal	crescent stitch, Max width & 0.3 length, elongation 3 (about ½" long)		Stitch diagonal rows over the brown satin ground with the three different stitches and thread colors (Project #4, page 48).
rust	feather leaf stitch, 5.0 width & 0.5 length		
gold metallic with black	asterisk stitch, Max width & Max length		
bronze	rickrack stitch, 2.5 width & 3.0 length	Couch 6 rows of medium brown yarn, ending at different heights (Project #1, page 37).	
	hollow leaf with stem stitch, Max width & Max length	Stitch 6 rows ending at different heights (Project #5, page 52). Mirror the stitch or turn the fabric so the leaves are pointing up.	
orange	punch work stitch, Max width & Max length	Stitch 6 rows ending at different heights. (Project #5, page 52).	
variegated brown	asterisk stitch, Max width & Max length	Stitch 6 rows ending at different heights. (Project #2, page 38).	

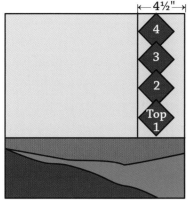

Satin squares placement

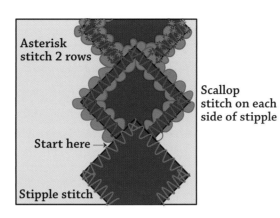

Asterisk stitch 2 rows

Scallop stitch on each side of stipple

Start here →

Stipple stitch

Stitch placement

Thread Color	Stitch Selection	Brown Satin Squares	Ground
Refer to project #3 (pages 43–45) for stitching techniques.			
bronze	stipple stitch, Max width & 1.0 length	Place 4 brown satin squares 2½" x 2½". Stitch around the edges of the squares as shown.	
dark teal	scallop stitch, Max width & 0.2 length, elongation 1 (about ¼" long)	Stitch around both sides of the bronze stipple stitching.	
rust	asterisk stitch, Max width & Max length	Stitch 2 rows over the previous stitching as shown.	Stitch a grid pattern on the medium brown ground (Project #3, page 44).

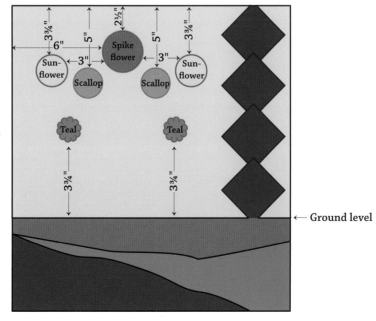

Flower placement

Ground level →

Thread Color	Stitch Selection	Spike Flower
Refer to project #3 (pages 42–45) for stitching techniques.		
orange	asterisk stitch, 3.0 width & 0.3 length	Place a brown satin circle 2½" in diameter for the Spike flower center as shown and stitch a ¼" grid pattern.
dark green	stem stitch, Max width & 0.3 length	Stitch a stem to brown center.
	grass stitch, Max width & 0.3 length	Cut 6 leaves (template, page 45). Place 3 pairs of leaves on the stem. Stitch around each leaf with the uneven edge of the stitch pointing out.
rust	petal stitch, Max width & 1" length, elongation 5 (about 1½" long)	Stitch petals around the flower center.
Variegated peach	grass stitch, Max width & 0.3 length	Stitch 2 rows around the flower center with the flat edges back-to-back. See Project #4, page 47.

Thread Color	Stitch Selection	Sunflowers
Refer to project #6 (pages 54–57) for stitching techniques.		
variegated forest green	diamond satin stitch, Max width & 3.0 length	Place 2 medium-brown with gold print circles 2" in diameter for the Sunflower centers as shown. Stitch the stems.
	solid leaf stitch, Max width & 1" length, single pattern stitch	Stitch leaves along the stem, curving them up at the ends.
gold metallic with black	scallop stitch, Max width & 0.3 length, elongation 1 (about ¼" long)	Stitch around the centers with the scalloped edge facing out.
rust	grass stitch, 4.0 width & 0.3 length	Stitch back-to-back with the scallop stitching.

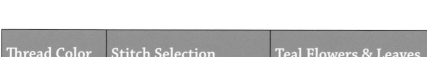

Thread Color	Stitch Selection	Teal Flowers & Leaves
Refer to project #2 (pages 38–41) for stitching techniques.		
gold metallic with black	stem stitch, 4.0 width & 2.0 length	Cut 2 flowers from the teal fabric using the smaller template (page 41) and place as shown. Stitch the stems.
	solid leaf stitch, Max width & 1" long, single pattern stitch	Stitch leaves along the stem.
rust	rickrack stitch, 3.5 width & 1.0 length	Stitch around the flower shapes.
	petal stitch, Max width & ⅜" long, single pattern stitch	Stitch the flower center.
gold metallic with black	grass stitch, Max width & 0.3 length	Stitch detail around the flower center.

Thread Color	Stitch Selection	Spiral Scallop Flowers & Background Plants
Refer to project #5 (pages 50–53) for stitching techniques.		
dark green	satin zigzag stitch, Max width & 0.2 length, elongation 1 (about ¼" long)	Draw a circle 1¾" in diameter for the scallop flowers in the position shown. Stitch a double stem.
	petal stitch, Max width & 1¼" long, elongation 5	Stitch a pair of leaves near the top of the stem.
rust	scallop stitch, Max width & 0.2 length, elongation 1 (about ¼" long)	Stitch around the circle from the outside in with the scallop edge facing out. You may want to iron flat.
	solid leaf with stem stitch, Max width & 0.3 length	Stitch 10 rows of background flowers ending at different heights.
dark teal		Stitch 9 rows of background flowers ending at different heights.

Twisted/Gathered Yarn Technique

Couch 3 rows of the brown, orange, and teal yarn along the edges of the ground fabrics (page 31).

Finishing

Finish as desired (page 32).

Project #7 SUNFLOWER #2, 10½" x 10½", made by the author

Project #7 SUNFLOWER #2

We will use a filler stitch on this project and add more fabric-layered shapes for design interest, plus we will be using an onion bag for added texture.

Materials

2 squares 12" x 12" medium-weight stabilizer

11" x 11" low-loft batting

11" x 11" bright yellow w/gold metallic
    pattern—foundation fabric

4" x 11" rust with gold sparkles—ground fabric

3" x 7" chocolate brown satin

   Cut 5 squares 1¼" x 1¼"

   Cut 1 circle 3" in diameter.

2½" x 11" red/orange onion bag (optional)

Threads

Copper metallic

Orange

Variegated forest
    green

Yellow/gold

Yarns

Brown

Orange

Yellow

Stitches

Asterisk

Grass

Feather

Feather leaf

Hollow diamond

Rickrack

Scallop

Stem

Stipple

Foundation & Fabric Placement

Thread the machine with yellow/gold thread and prepare the foundation fabric with 2 squares of stabilizer (page 29) using the asterisk stitch, Max width & Max length. Push the fabric as you sew with an even pressure to allow a slight distortion.

Place the rust fabric and red onion bag as shown. Using the same yellow/gold thread, select stipple stitch, Max width minus 0.5 with the feed dogs down, giving you control over the length. Stipple stitch the ground fabrics. Raise feed dogs when finished.

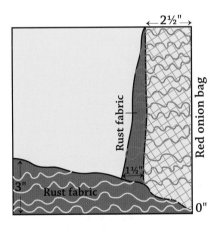

Ground fabric and stipple stitch placement

Add plants and squares as follows:

Thread Color	Stitch Selection	Circle Flower & Brown Squares
yellow/gold	rickrack stitch, 3.5 width & 2.0 length	Place the 3" circle and 5 brown 1¼" squares as shown. Starting at the edge of the brown circle, spiral in to the center keeping the rows of stitches next to each other. When you get closer to the center you will be spinning the fabric. Allow the stitches to curve and distort. Make the center more dense by overlapping several times.
	stipple stitch, Max width & 1.6 length	Stitch around the edges of the brown squares as shown.

½" from edge of squares

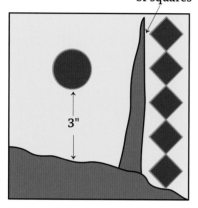

Fabric placement and stipple stitching placement on squares

See chart, page 67.

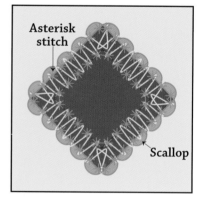

Fern placement

Brown square stitch placement

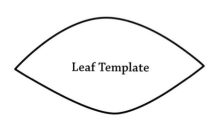

Leaf Template

Twisted/Gathered Yarn Technique

Couch yellow, orange, and brown yarn along the edge of the three ground fabrics (page 31).

Finishing

Finish as desired (page 32).

Thread Color	Stitch Selection	Circle Flower & Brown Squares	Ground
variegated forest green	stem stitch, Max width & 0.3 length	Stitch a stem for the circle flower.	
	stipple stitch, Max width & 1.0 length	Draw 2 pairs of leaves using the template (page 45) and stitch around inside the lines, overlapping the first layer as you spiral into the center.	
	grass stitch, Max width & 0.3 length	Stitch on the line at the outside edge of the leaves with the uneven edge facing in.	
	feather stitch, Max width & 0.5 length		Stitch between the rows of yellow stipple stitching on the rust fabrics.
	asterisk stitch, Max width & Max length		Stitch a line around the brown squares ⅜" beyond their edges.
orange	scallop stitch, Max width & 0.3 length, elongation 1 (about ¼" long)	With the scalloped edge facing out, stitch around the flower center starting ⅛" beyond the edge, then spiral in ⅛" and stitch over the first layer. Stitch 3 layers.	
		Stitch around the edges of the brown squares with the scalloped edge facing out.	
	hollow diamond stitch, Max width & 2.0 length		Stitch a curvy line between the feather stitching on the ground, overlapping the yellow stipple stitches.
copper metallic	grass stitch, Max width & 0.3 length	Stitch along the inside of the flower scallops stitching back-to-back with the uneven edge facing in.	
	feather leaf stitch, Max width & 1¼" long, single pattern stitch	Turn the quilt so the ground is at the top and stitch 4 rows curving to one side. Mirror image or flip and stitch 4 more rows back-to-back with the first, curving in the opposite direction. You may need to mirror the stitch so the wide end stitches out first. See fern placement on page 66.	
	asterisk stitch, Max width & Max length	Stitch along the edge of the stipple stitching on the brown squares. Stitch 2 rows.	

Project #8 PINE TREE #1, 10½" x 10½", made by the author

Project #8 PINE TREE #1

We will use craft felt and filler stitches on this project, and add stitching to create wind and snow.

Materials

2 squares 12" x 12" medium-weight stabilizer
11" x 11" low-loft batting
11" x 11" white-on-white—foundation
5" x 11" brown w/green dots—ground
8" x 8" olive green craft felt—trees

Threads

Brown
Dark green
Eggshell
Metallic ivory
Variegated grass
    green
Variegated sky blue

Yarns

Brown
Green
Ivory

Stitches

Asterisk
Grass
Rickrack
Stem
Stipple

Foundation

Thread the machine with eggshell thread and prepare the foundation fabric with 2 squares of stabilizer (page 29) using the rickrack stitch, 5.0 width with the feed dogs dropped, which gives you control over the length. Raise the feed dogs when finished.

Wind and snow stitching

Add trees, wind, and ground cover as follows:

Thread Color	Stitch Selection	Background Wind and Snow
variegated sky blue	rickrack stitch, 3.5 width & 4. 0 length	Starting at the left edge, stitch 9 rows of "wind" across the foundation.
metallic ivory	asterisk stitch, Max width & Max length	Stitch 8 rows of "snow."

Thread Color	Stitch Selection	Ground
metallic ivory	asterisk stitch, Max width & Max length	Cut and place the ground fabric as shown. Stitch big, funky figure eights as shown.
dark green		Repeat figure eights.

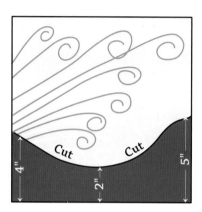 

Ground fabric and asterisk stitch placement

Thread Color	Stitch Selection	Trees
dark green	stipple stitch, Max width & 1.6 length	Using the templates provided (page 71) cut one large tree and 2 smaller trees from green craft felt. Position them. Start at the top of the large tree and stipple stitch each section in a spiral from the outside in. Repeat on all trees. See diagram on page 71.
variegated grass green	stem stitch, Max width & 0.3 length	Stitch on the diagonal across the body of the trees every ½".
brown		Stitch 3 rows, side-by-side and overlapping the middle row to create the tree trunks.
dark green	grass stitch, Max width & 0.3 length	Stitch around the trees with the flat side of the stitching along the edge and the uneven side facing out. Start at the bottom section, then overlap the next section's stitching. Repeat on all 3 trees.

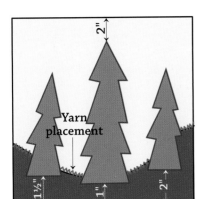

Tree placement

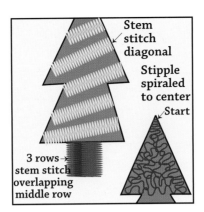
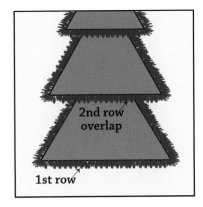

Stitch placement

Twisted/Gathered Yarn Technique

Couch brown, ivory, and green yarn, and stitch along the ground level in between the trees (page 31).

Finishing

Finish as desired (page 32).

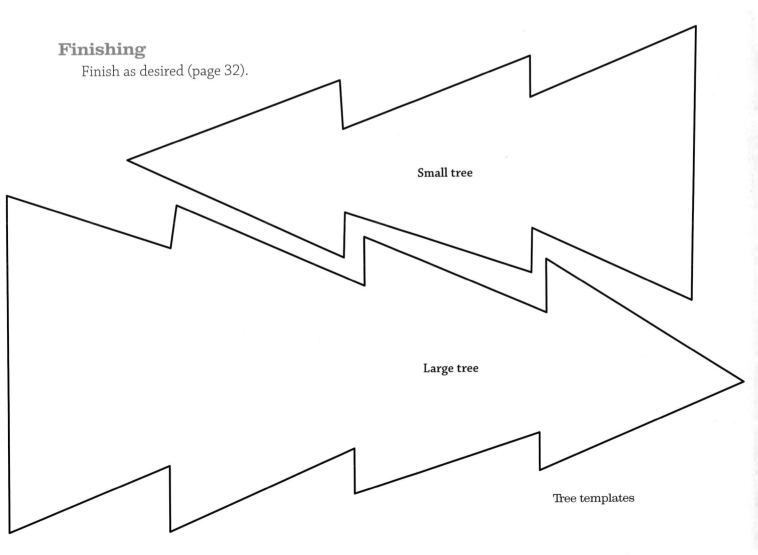

Small tree

Large tree

Tree templates

Project #9 PINE TREE #2, 10½" x 10½", made by the author

Project #9 PINE TREE #2

This project includes a tree base of tulle and velveteen, couching yarn, and stitching a fun weaving technique for the ground.

Materials

2 squares 12" x 12" medium-weight stabilizer
11" x 11" low-loft batting
11" x 11" peach w/yellow—foundation
9" x 2" brown velveteen—tree trunk
5" x 7" green velvet—ground
4" x 6" green satin—ground
7" x 14" black tulle—tree

Threads / Stitches

Threads	Stitches
Brown	Asterisk
Dark green	Blanket
Orange	Crescent
Variegated meadow green	Cross
	Stem
Variegated peach	Stipple

Yarns

Brown
Green bulky
Green eyelash

Foundation

Thread the machine with variegated peach thread and prepare the foundation fabric with 2 squares of stabilizer (page 29) using the blanket stitch, Max width minus .05 & 4.0 length. Drop the feed dogs, which gives you control over the length. Raise the feed dogs when finished.

Ground and Tree Fabric Placement

Place cut tree and ground fabrics as shown. The green velvet should overlap the green satin. Place the end of the tree trunk under the edge of the ground. Fold the tulle to measure 7" x 7". Place over the trunk, pin down the middle, and trim as shown.

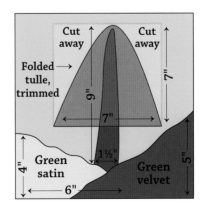

Ground and tree fabric placement

Add ground and tree stitches as follows:

Thread Color	Stitch Selection	Ground
variegated peach	asterisk stitch, Max width & 0.3 length	Stitch an X pattern on the green velvet.
	stem stitch, Max width & 0.3 length	Stitch a ¾" grid basket weave pattern on the green satin.

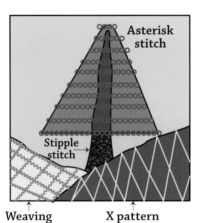

Ground and tree stitching placement

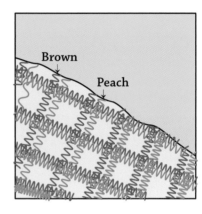

Additional ground stitching placement

Thread Color	Stitch Selection	Ground	Tree
brown	stipple stitch, Max width & 2.0 length		Stitch the tree trunk from the tulle to the ground. Stippling on the velvet creates a perfect bumpy bark texture.
	asterisk stitch, Max width & Max length	Stitch an X pattern on the green velvet, offsetting the lines from the previous stitching.	Stitch 10 rows 1" apart across the tree using the tulle as the template, starting and ending with one stitch pattern beyond the tulle.
	stem stitch, 4.0 width & 0.3 length	Stitch a weaving pattern on the green satin to the left of the peach stem stitching, leaving ⅛" space.	

Thread Color	Stitch Selection	Ground	Tree
dark green	cross-stitch, Max width & 3.0 length		Couch 10 rows of bulky green yarn directly below the brown asterisk stitching.
	asterisk stitch, Max width & Max length	Stitch an X pattern on the green velvet, offsetting the lines from the previous stitching.	
	stem stitch, 4.0 width & 0.3 length	Stitch a weaving pattern on the green satin next to the brown stem stitching, leaving ⅛" space.	
variegated meadow green	stem stitch, Max width & 0.3 length		Stitch 10 rows above the brown asterisk stitching.
	asterisk stitch, Max width & Max length	Stitch an X pattern on the green velvet, offsetting the lines from the previous stitching.	
	stem stitch, 4.0 width & 0.3 length	Stitch a weaving pattern on the green satin next to the dark green stem stitching, leaving ⅛" space.	
orange	crescent stitch, Max width & 0.3 length, elongation 1 (about ¼" long)		Stitch 9 rows across beneath the couched green yarn.
	asterisk stitch, Max width & Max length	Stitch an X pattern on the green velvet, offsetting the lines from the previous stitching.	
	stem stitch, 4.0 width & 0.3 length	Stitch a weaving pattern on the green satin next to the meadow green stem stitching, leaving ⅛" space.	

Twisted/Gathered Yarn Technique

Couch brown, green eyelash, and green bulky yarn, stitch along the green satin ground, then along the green velvet (page 31).

Finishing

Finish as desired (page 32).

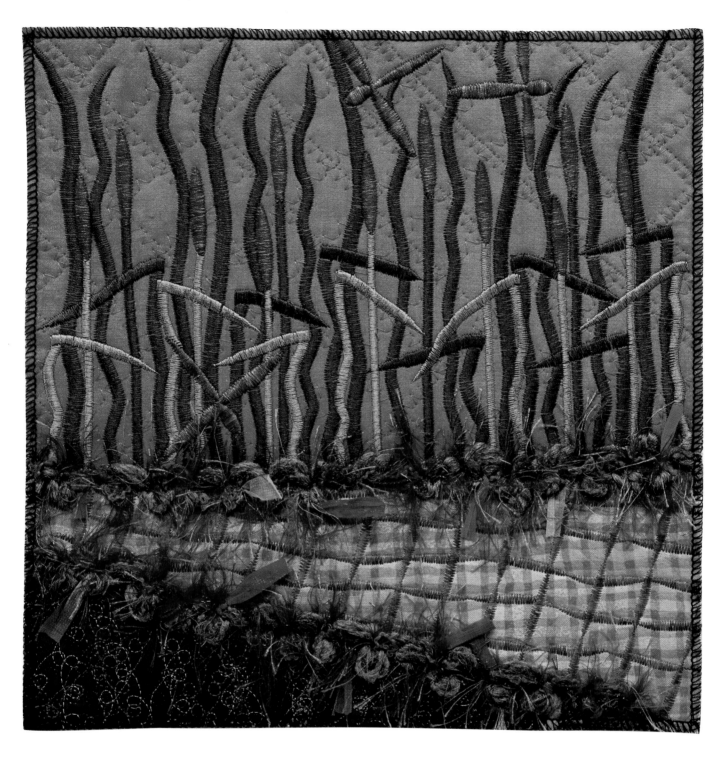

Project #10 CATTAILS WITH DRAGONFLIES, 10½" x 10½", made by the author

Project #10 CATTAILS WITH DRAGONFLIES

In this project we will use the tapering technique. (Refer to the tapering details, page 18.) We will use the petal stitch to create the dragonflies.

Materials

2 squares 12" x 12" medium-weight stabilizer
11" x 11" low-loft batting
11" x 11" solid dark pink—foundation
11" x 4" light blue with blue check pattern—ground
11" x 4" dark purple—ground

Threads
Dark green
Dark pink
Medium green
Variegated purple
Variegated royal
    blue

Stitches
Blanket
Loop
Petal
Zigzag

Yarns
Blue with pink
    accents
Green
Purple

Foundation

Thread the machine with dark pink thread and prepare the foundation fabric with 2 squares of stabilizer (page 29) using the blanket stitch at the default setting. Push the fabric as you're sewing to distort the stitches.

Ground

Place the dark purple fabric at the bottom of the foundation. Cut the light blue fabric and place on top.

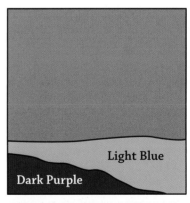

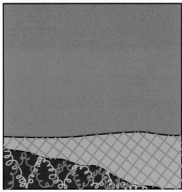

Ground and stitching placement

Add the cattails, dragonflies, and ground cover as follows:

Thread Color	Stitch Selection	Cattails and Dragonflies	Ground
dark pink	loop stitch, default setting		Stitch an overall pattern on the purple ground fabric as shown.
variegated royal blue	petal stitch, 4.0 width & 0.4 length, elongation 5 (about 1" long)		Stitch diagonal rows on the light-blue ground ½" apart; repeat in the opposite direction to create a grid.
dark green	zigzag stitch, Max width & 0.2 length	Practice tapering before sewing on your quilt. Starting at the ground, stitch 5 curvy rows about 2¼" apart, ending each with a tapered point ½" from the top. Stitch 8 curvy rows ending each with a tapered point 1" from the top.	
	zigzag stitch, 6.0 width & 0.2 length	Stitch 4 straight rows for the stalks, ending 4½" from the top. Do not taper these rows. Stitch 7 rows from 3"–4" tall. Stop with the needle down on the opposite side of the direction you wish the leaf to bend. Pivot and stitch on a diagonal downward to a tapered point. Practice this on a test sheet.	
	loop stitch, default setting		Stitch an overall pattern on the purple ground.
medium green	loop stitch, default setting		Stitch an overall pattern on the purple ground.
	zigzag stitch, 3.5 width & 0.2 length	Stitch 7 straight rows 3"–3½" long. Fit them between the dark green leaves. It is OK to stitch on top of previous leaves. Do not taper these rows.	
	zigzag stitch, 5.0 width & 0.2 length	Stitch 6–7 curvy rows at different heights. Needle down, pivot, and stitch on a diagonal downward to a tapered point.	
variegated purple	petal stitch, Max width & 1.25" length, single stitch pattern, elongation 5 (about 1½")	Rotate the quilt 180 degrees and stitch a petal at the top of each dark-green and medium-green stem. Start ¼" onto the stalk and stitch out a single stitch pattern. Pivot and stitch over as many times as desired to make the cattail tops.	
	loop stitch, default setting		Stitch an overall pattern on the purple ground.

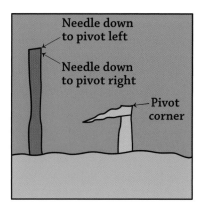

Needle down
to pivot left

Needle down
to pivot right

Pivot
corner

Pivot to stitch top of bent leaves.

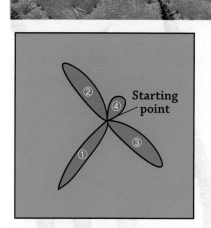

② ④ Starting
point

①

③

Dragonfly
Starting point in center,
stitch out tail ①,
wing ②, wing ③, head ④

Thread Color	Stitch Selection	Cattails and Dragonflies	Ground
variegated royal blue	petal stitch, 5.0 width, elongation 5 (about 1" long)	Pick a starting point. Stitch the dragonfly body. Pivot and stitch back to the starting point. Change the width to 6.0 and stitch the wings, pivoting at the ends and stitching back to the starting point. Change the length to 0.2, elongation 3 (about ½" long) and stitch the head. Repeat for as many dragonflies as desired.	

Twisted/Gathered Yarn Technique

Couch 2 rows of the green, purple, and blue with pink yarn along the ground edges (page 31).

Finishing

Finish as desired (page 32).

Project #11 FORGET-ME-NOT, 10½" x 10½", made by the author

Project #11 FORGET-ME-NOT

In this project we will create a forget-me-not plant with the crescent stitch, which starts and ends at the same point. This technique will take a little practice, but it is worth the effort to make this cute little flower.

Materials

2 squares 12" x 12" medium-weight stabilizer
11" x 11" low-loft batting
11" x 11" orange—foundation
3" x 11" dark blue with darker blue print—ground

Threads

Dark blue
Dark green
Medium orange
Variegated royal
  blue

Stitches

Crescent
Cross
Diamond satin
Petal
Zigzag

Yarns

Dark blue
Medium blue
Orange

Foundation

Thread the machine with medium-orange thread and prepare the foundation fabric with 2 squares of stabilizer (page 29) using the cross-stitch, Max width & Max length. Push the fabric quickly as you're sewing to distort the stitches.

Ground

Place the 3" x 11" dark-blue rectangle along the bottom of the foundation fabric.

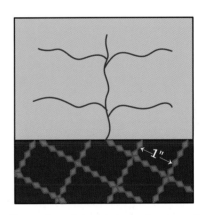

Ground and main stem placement

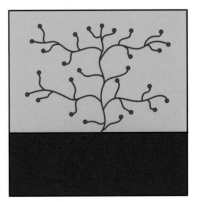

Adding stems

Add the plant and ground cover as follows:

Thread Color	Stitch Selection	Forget-Me-Not	Ground
orange	diamond satin stitch, Max width & 0.2, elongation 3 (about ½" long)		Stitch rows on the diagonal 1" apart; repeat in the opposite direction to create a grid.
dark green	zigzag stitch, 3.0 & 0.2	Draw 5 lines for the main stems. Add as many stems off the main ones as you like. You'll stitch a flower at the end of each stem. Stitch over the lines to create the stems.	
	diamond satin stitch, Max width & 0.3 length, elongation 3 (about ½" long)		Stitch a row ¼" to the right of the previous grid stitching.
variegated royal blue	diamond satin stitch, Max width & 0.3 length, elongation 3 (about ½" long)		Stitch a row ¼" to the right of the previous grid stitching.
	crescent stitch, Max width, 1" long, elongation 5 (about 1" long)	Practice this on your test sheet before you stitch on the quilt. Start stitching at the end of a stem, pull the fabric sideways, then back to the starting spot. Repeat 3 times for a total of 4 petals for each flower. Stitch a flower at the end of each stem.	

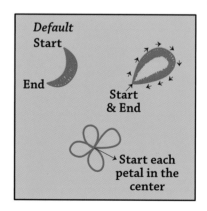

Stitching petals by altering the crescent stitch

Thread Color	Stitch Selection	Forget-Me-Not	Ground
dark green	petal stitch, Max width & 1" long, single pattern stitch, elongation 5 (about 1" long)	Stitch leaves out from the stems, pivot, and stitch back to the stem, placing leaves in areas needing fill.	
dark blue	diamond satin stitch, 6.0 width & 0.3 length, single pattern stitch, elongation 1 (about ¼" long)	Stitch a diamond in the center of each flower. Pivot and stitch over multiple times to create a denser, puffier center.	

Twisted/Gathered Yarn Technique

Couch the medium blue, dark blue, and orange yarn along the ground (page 31).

Finishing

Finish as desired (page 32).

Project #12 ULTRASUEDE VINE, 10½" x 10½", made by the author

Project #12 **ULTRASUEDE VINE**

We will be using Ultrasuede® fabric in this project. If you can not find Ultrasuede in your area, you can use any polar fleece or craft felt.

Materials

2 squares 12" x 12" medium-weight stabilizer

11" x 11" low-loft batting

11" x 11" gold with small print—foundation

6" x 10" brown velveteen—ground and circles
  Cut ground piece and 4 circles 2" in diameter as shown.

3" x 11" hot pink with small print—ground
  Cut in half on the diagonal as shown.

4" x 8" hot pink Ultrasuede,
  Cut 8 circles 1¼" in diameter.
  Cut 6 circles ¾" in diameter.

3" x 6" medium green Ultrasuede
  Cut 16 leaves from the template (below).

2" x 6" gold/yellow Ultrasuede
  Cut 8 circles 1" in diameter.

Threads

Brown

Green

Hot pink

Variegated dark brown

Variegated peach

Yarns

Brown

Green

Hot pink

Stitches

Asterisk

Petal

Rickrack

Scallop

Stem

Stipple

Foundation

Thread the machine with the variegated peach thread and prepare the foundation fabric with 2 squares of stabilizer (page 29) using the stipple stitch, Max width & 5.0 length. Push the fabric as you're sewing to distort the stitches.

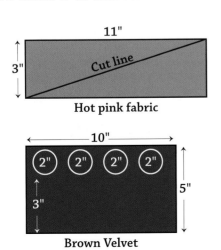

Hot pink fabric

Brown Velvet

Leaf Template

Ground

Place the brown velvet and pink triangles as shown.

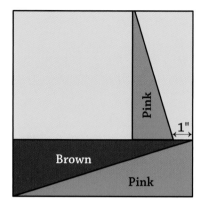
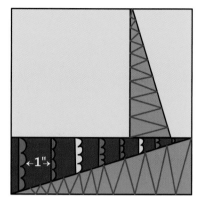

Ground and stitching placement

Add flowers, hanging vines, and ground cover as follows:

Thread Color	Stitch Selection	Ground
variegated peach hot pink	scallop stitch, Max width & 0.3 length, elongation 1 (about ¼" long)	Stitch rows 1" apart on the brown velvet ground. Repeat with the remaining 3 colors, stitching rows ¼" to the right of the previous stitching.
dark green variegated dark brown	asterisk stitch, Max width & Max length	Stitch a large W pattern on both areas of hot pink. Repeat with the remaining 3 colors, offsetting from the precious stitching.

Brown circle placement

Brown velvet circle stitching placement

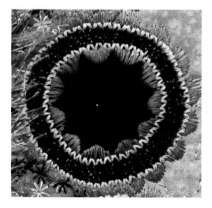

Thread Color	Stitch Selection	Flowers
variegated dark brown	stipple stitch, Max width & 1.6 length	Center the brown circles on the right edge of the hot pink fabric. Stitch around the edges.
hot pink	scallop stitch, Max width & 0.3 length, elongation 1 (about ¼" long)	Stitch around both sides of the stipple stitching with the scalloped edges facing away from the stipple stitching.
variegated peach	rickrack stitch, 2.5 width & 1.0 length	Stitch a row along the straight edge of the scallop stitching.

Thread Color	Stitch Selection	Hanging Vines
dark green	stem stitch, Max width & 0.3 length	Draw 3 curvy lines for the vine stems as shown. Stitch over the drawn lines to form the stems.
hot pink	petal stitch, Max width & 0.2 length, single pattern stitch, elongation 1 (about ¼" long)	Position the 1¼" hot pink circles on the stems as shown and place the 1" gold circles on top of them. Secure with a single pattern in the center, offsetting the starting point.
dark green	rickrack stitch, 2.5 width & 1.0 length	Position 2 leaves on opposite sides of the circle flowers. Stitch down the center of each leaf.
	petal stitch, Max width & ¾" long, single pattern stitch, elongation 5 (about 1" long)	Stitch pairs of leaves on the stems between the flowers.
variegated peach	petal stitch, Max width & ½" long, single pattern stitch, elongation 1 (about ½" long)	Position the ¾" circles between the stitched leaves. Secure with a single pattern in the center, offsetting the starting point.

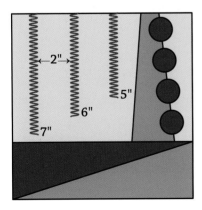

Hanging vine stem placement

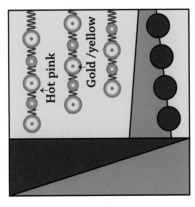

Pink and gold Ultrasuede circle placement

Twisted/Gathered Yarn Technique

Couch the hot pink, medium green, and gold/yellow yarn along the ground edges and the left side of the brown circle/hot pink section (page 31).

Finishing

Finish as desired (page 32).

FOREST FROLIC, 18" x 19", made by the author

FOREST FROLIC

This is a fun project that combines the techniques used in projects #7 through #12. We will be referring back to each project for design and techniques.

Materials

2 squares 21" x 21" medium-weight stabilizer

19" x 19" low-loft batting

19" x 19" pale green with small pattern—foundation

7" x 14" green velvet—ground and vertical accent

2¼" x 25", rust with sparkles—ground and three 1¼" circles for the sunflowers

3" x 30" orange, yellow & green marbled—ground and 4 accent circles 2½" in diameter

5" x 16" black tulle—tree

6" x 8½" green craft felt—tree

10" x 2" brown velveteen—tree trunk

Foundation

Thread the machine with pale green thread and prepare the foundation fabric with 2 squares of stabilizer (page 29) using the blanket stitch, Max width & Max length. Push the fabric as you're sewing to distort the stitches.

Ground

Place the rust and marbled fabrics on the foundation.

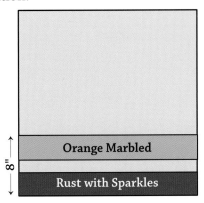

Orange and rust fabric placement

Threads	Yarns	Stitches
Brown	Brown	Asterisk
Copper metallic	Green bulky	Blanket
Dark green	Orange	Crescent
Medium green		Cross
Pale green		Diamond satin
Rust		Grass
Variegated dark brown		Loop
Variegated forest green		Petal
Variegated meadow green		Rickrack
Yellow/gold		Scallop
		Stem
		Stipple
		Zigzag

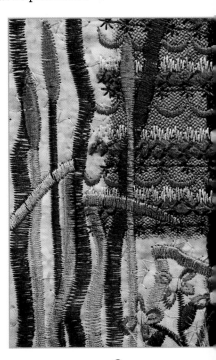

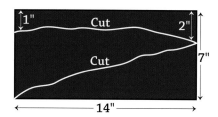

Cut 3 pieces from the green velvet and place them as shown.

Green velvet cutting diagram

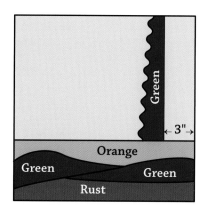

Green velvet placement

Add design elements as follows:

Thread Color	Stitch Selection	Ground—refer to Project #10 (pages 76–79)
all thread colors	loop stitch, Max width & Max length	Each time you load a new thread color, stitch a "W" pattern across the green velvet accent and ground pieces, offsetting the stitching each time.

Thread Color	Stitch Selection	Ground—refer to Project #11 (pages 80–83)
brown	diamond satin stitch, Max width & 0.3 length, elongation 1 (about ¼" long)	Stitch uneven rows on the diagonal 1" apart on the orange marble ground; repeat in the opposite direction to create a grid. *Note: I did not do a true grid on this project. Notice how it changes the look of the pattern.*
dark green		Repeat the uneven grid on the orange marble ground, centering the stitches between the brown diamonds.

Thread Color	Stitch Selection	Ground—refer to Project #9 (pages 72–75)
dark green	stem stitch, Max width & 0.3 length	Stitch a 1" grid basket weave pattern on the rust ground.
brown		Stitch a second layer grid on the rust ground project.

Forget-me-not flower design

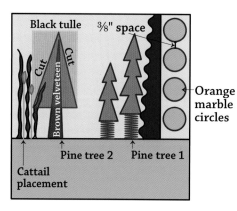

Circles, trees, and cattails placement

Sunflower and forget-me-not placement

YOUR MACHINE'S DECORATIVE *STITCHES* ❄ *Karen Linduska*

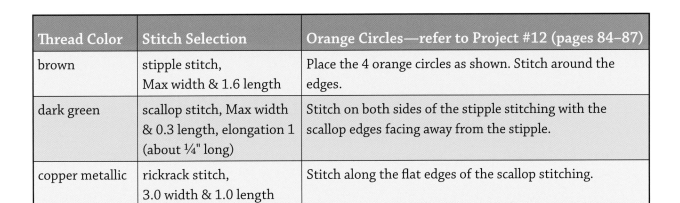

Thread Color	Stitch Selection	Orange Circles—refer to Project #12 (pages 84–87)
brown	stipple stitch, Max width & 1.6 length	Place the 4 orange circles as shown. Stitch around the edges.
dark green	scallop stitch, Max width & 0.3 length, elongation 1 (about ¼" long)	Stitch on both sides of the stipple stitching with the scallop edges facing away from the stipple.
copper metallic	rickrack stitch, 3.0 width & 1.0 length	Stitch along the flat edges of the scallop stitching.

Thread Color	Stitch Selection	Pine Tree #1—refer to Project #8 (pages 68–71)
dark green	stipple stitch, Max width & 1.6 length	Use the templates (page 93) to cut 1 small and 1 large pine tree from the craft felt and position. Stitch a filler layer on the trees.
variegated dark brown	stem stitch, Max width & 0.3 length	Stitch 3 rows side by side for the tree trunks.
variegated meadow green		Stitch diagonal rows across the trees 1" apart.
dark green	grass stitch, Max width & 0.3 length	Outline all sections of the trees with the uneven edge of the stitching facing out.

Thread Color	Stitch Selection	Pine Tree #2—refer to Project #9 (pages 72–75)
brown	stipple stitch, Max width & 1.6 length	Cut a trunk from the brown velveteen and place. Fold the tulle in half to measure 5" x 8". Position over the trunk, pin down the middle, and trim as shown. Stitch an overall pattern on the part of the trunk extending below the tulle.
	asterisk stitch, Max width & 1.6 length	Stitch 9 rows 1" apart across the tree using the tulle as the template, starting and ending with one stitch pattern beyond the tulle.
dark green	cross-stitch, Max width & 3.0 length	Couch 9 rows of bulky green yarn above each row of asterisk stitches.
variegated meadow green	stem stitch, Max width & 0.3 length	Stitch 8 rows next to the couched yarn.
rust	crescent stitch, Max width & 0.2 length, elongation 3 (about ½" long)	Stitch 8 rows between the asterisk and stem stitches.

Thread Color	Stitch Selection	Cattails—refer to Project #10 (pages 76–79)
dark green	zigzag stitch, Max width & 0.2 length	Stitch 3 tall curvy leaves of different heights, tapering to a point (manually or using your machine's taper feature).
	zigzag stitch, 3.5 width & 0.2 length	Stitch one straight stem (no tapering).
medium green	zigzag stitch, 3.5 width & 0.2 length	Stitch 2 straight stems (no tapering).
	zigzag stitch, 5.5 width & 0.2 length	Stitch 3 curvy stems of different heights (no tapering).
		Stitch bent leaves onto the curvy stems, stitching on a downward diagonal.
rust	petal stitch, Max width, 1.25" long	Stitch cattail tops onto the 3 straight, untapered stems, 2 layers of stitching each.

Thread Color	Stitch Selection	Sunflowers—refer to Project #7 (pages 64–67)
yellow/gold	rickrack stitch, 3.0 width & 1.3 length	Place the 3 rust 1¼" circles. Stitch a spiral from the edges to the center.
variegated forest green	stem stitch, Max width & 0.3 length	Stitch a stem for each sunflower.
	stipple stitch, Max width & 1.0 length	Using the leaf template below, draw 2 pairs of leaves on each stem. Fill in the leaves.
	grass stitch, Max width & 0.3 length	Outline the leaves with the uneven edge of the grass stitch facing in.
copper metallic	scallop stitch, Max width & 0.2 length, elongation 1 (about ¼" long)	Starting ⅛" from edge of flower center, stitch 3 layers around the flowers with the scalloped edge facing out.

Once you have stitched the Forget-Me-Not from page 93, proceed as follows:

Leaf Template

Twisted/Gathered Yarn Technique

Couch bulky green, orange, and brown yarn along the edges of the ground sections (page 31).

Finishing

Finish as desired (page 32).

Thread Color	Stitch Selection	Forget-Me-Not—refer to Project #11 (pages 80–83)
dark green	zigzag stitch, 2.5 width & 0.3 length	Draw in the stems, filling in the ground level area. (I drew 6 flowers.) Stitch over the drawn lines.
	petal stitch, 7.0 width & ½" long, single pattern stitch, elongation 3 (about ½" long)	Stitch 3–4 leaves per plant.
rust	crescent stitch, Max width & 0.3 length, single pattern stitch, elongation 5 (about 1" long)	Stitch 4 petals per stem, turning the fabric so the petals begin and end at the same spot.
yellow/gold	petal stitch, 6.0 width & 0.2 length, single pattern stitch, elongation 1 (about ¼" long)	Stitch one pattern on the horizontal in the center of each flower.

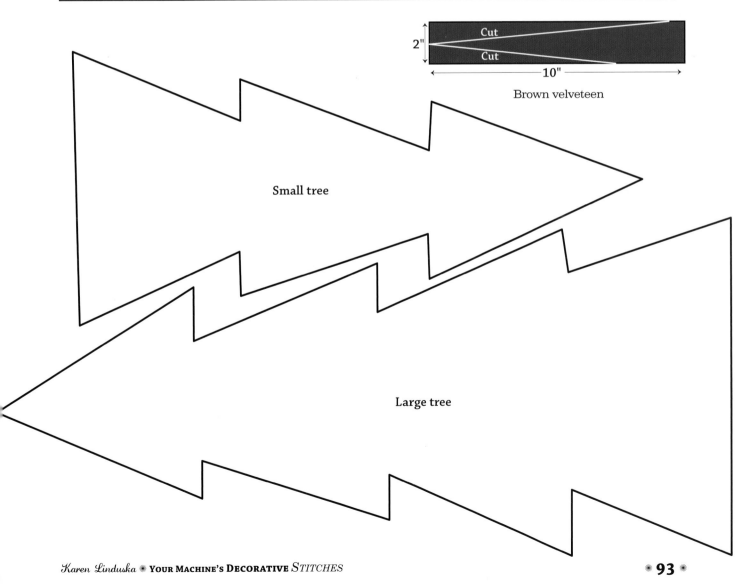

Small tree

Large tree

Cut

Cut

2"

10"

Brown velveteen

Resources

KAREN LINDUSKA

www.karenlinduska.com

Go to my web page to view my quilt galleries.

www.karenlinduska. blogspot.com

My blog has current class and lecture information and current postings related to my machine embroidery process. I invite you to become a fan of my Facebook page, and Decorative Stitch Thread Painting with Karen Linduska.

BABY LOCK

www.babylock.com

Baby Lock sewing machines are very user-friendly. Check out their site for current information.

THREAD ART

www.threadart.com

800-504-6867

This is a great source for items you want to buy in bulk such as thread and pre-wound bobbins.

YLI CORPORATION

1439 Dave Lyle Boulevard
Rock Hill, SC 29730

www.ylicorp.com

This company has great thread. Check out their site for their entire product line.

FAIRFIELD PROCESSING CORPORATION

www.poly-fil.com/

This is a great site for information about Fairfield Quilt Batting.

NANCY'S NOTIONS

www.nancysnotions.com

333 Beichl Avenue
Beaver Dam, WI

CALICO COUNTRY SEW & VAC

310 South Logan/Route 37 South
West Frankfort, IL
618-932-2992

2525 Fairview Drive
Carbondale, IL 62901
618-529-5665

Both locations are a treasure trove of goodies related to sewing. Plan on spending some time there. They have it all.

HELENE'S HAND-DYED FABRICS

www.hand-dye.com

1149 Jefferson Street
Paducah, KY

The colors of Helene Davis' hand-dyed fabrics are beautiful and a lovely addition to your art quilts.

Meet **Karen Linduska**

I consider myself very lucky to have discovered the fiber world at an early age. I was very content to spend time sewing, knitting, and making whatever inspired me. It never occurred to me to be anything but an artist. The fiber medium came to me early and we have been one ever since. I taught myself to sew on a machine around the age of ten. I am a born problem solver, so a lot of the challenges I came across only slowed me down slightly. I figured out what to do and kept moving forward.

My high school art teacher just happened to be a fiber artist, so fiber was what I focused on. I worked on projects that were very involved. It was at this time in my life that I developed the discipline it takes to create detailed works on fabric.

I majored in fibers at college and attended Southern Illinois University. I studied under M. Joan Lintault. Joan is one of the founding members of the art quilt movement and was a wealth of information. She was all about creating a foundation with the fiber medium—to learn how to do the basics and work up from there. This is where I learned to dye fabric and work on surface design. College for me was about working on content. I took this information and spent the next 30 years living and breathing fiber art.

Today I am a full-time award-winning fiber artist, author, and teacher and consider myself very lucky. I get to make art quilts for a living. I get to write about what I love to do. I get to teach in a field where people are happy and excited about learning. For me it's all about moving forward in a positive direction and sharing the knowledge that flows out of me.

other AQS Books

This is only a small selection of the books available from the American Quilter's Society. AQS books are known worldwide for timely topics, clear writing, beautiful color photos, and accurate illustrations and patterns. The following books are available from your local bookseller, quilt shop, or public library.

#8238   US $26.95

#7926   US $24.95

#8237   US $26.95

#8029   US $28.95

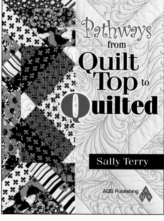

#8348   US $28.95

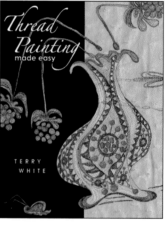

#7603   US $27.95

#8354   US $28.95

#7611   US $26.95

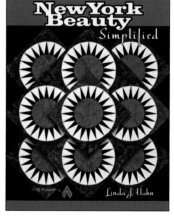

#8346   US $26.95

LOOK for these books nationally.
CALL or **VISIT** our website at

1-800-626-5420
www.AmericanQuilter.com